THE *NEW* CHRISTMAS EVERY DAY

ELY R. S.

WESTBOW
PRESS®
A DIVISION OF THOMAS NELSON
& ZONDERVAN

WestBow Press books may be ordered through booksellers or by contacting:

WestBow Press
A Division of Thomas Nelson & Zondervan
1663 Liberty Drive
Bloomington, IN 47403
www.westbowpress.com
1 (866) 928-1240

ISBN: 978-1-5127-1366-4 (sc)
ISBN: 978-1-5127-1367-1 (e)

Library of Congress Control Number: 2015915692

Print information available on the last page.

WestBow Press rev. date: 09/24/2015

Table of Contents

Dedication

This Christmas book is dedicated first and foremost
to the Birthday Celebrant- our dear Lord and
Savior Jesus Christ. And I'm grateful to my wife,
she is always on my side in my more than 30
years in the ministry. To God Be the Glory!

Foreword

I was privileged to visit Israel for the first time many years ago. I was excited and thrilled as I walked through the streets of Nazareth to visit the place of our Lord where He once lived. Nazareth was the hometown of Jesus. No wonder He was called Jesus of Nazareth in the scriptures. I remember standing on the hillside near Capernaum Peter's hometown. I could almost hear Jesus sharing the Beatitudes. I imagined Jesus sailing on the Sea of Galilee. I could feel Jesus' presence and heard His words and sensed His authority over the storm when He calmed the storm with His words. Outside the city of Sychar, I could almost see Jesus bringing a troubled woman to the living water. Jerusalem is the holy city and it was called the city of David, home to the temple and the place wherein Jesus came as a sacrifice for our sin (John 1:11; Romans 5:8; 6:23). I can feel the agony while I was walking in the Garden of Gethsemane where Jesus sweat drops of blood. I can feel the pain and the love of God as we climbed up to Mount Calvary where Jesus died on the cross.

Kneeling at the mouth of the empty tomb where Jesus conquered sin, death, and hell for us, and made our spirit and our soul at peace with Him. What an affirmation of the truths I had believed since I was a boy. It's a blessing to be right there and experienced the thrill of the reality of God's love. The greatest thrill was being in Bethlehem where eternal God stepped into time. Jesus became the son of man, so men could be sons of God. Without Bethlehem, there was no redemption. This was the fulfillment of all the Old Testament prophecies and symbols, etc. *"But as for you Bethlehem…One will go forth for Me to be the ruler in all Israel. His going forth are from long ago, from the days of eternity" (Micah 5:2).* As I stood in the grotto beneath the church of the Nativity on the very place where Jesus was born, we sang: *"O little town of Bethlehem, How still we see thee lie! Above thy deep and dreamless sleep the silent stars go by; yet in thy dark streets shineth the everlasting Light; The hopes and fears of all the years area meet in thee tonight."* Every time I sing this beautiful Christmas carol; I shed tears of joy from my eyes as I remember Bethlehem and the wonder of Christmas. I could only wish that every believer could have this experience.

Since this is impossible for most of us, I am so glad my dear friend and fellow pastor Ely R. S. has taken the time to research many wonderful things about this greatest event of all history- *Christmas*. I know you will enjoy the stories and the traditions of different countries concerning this glorious celebration called *Christmas*. I hope you will experience Christmas as if you were there in Bethlehem. I know the Lord has much to teach you through Pastor Ely. My prayer is that as you read this book that Christmas will become more personal and exciting to you. And if you have not personally experienced eternal life through faith in this Christ-child that became the sacrifice for our sin, that through this book you would come to know Jesus as your Lord and Savior.

Jimmy Jones

Education:
B.A. Wheaton College, Wheaton Illinois Masters of Divinity Southwestern Baptist Theological Seminary, Fort Worth, Texas

Ministries:
Pastor First Baptist Church Trenton 1960-1983, 1999-2012, State Director of Evangelism Baptist State Convention of Michigan 1983-1999

Denominational service:
President Baptist State Convention of Michigan, Trustee- Annuity Board SBC (Guidestone Financial Resources) Member Executive Committee SBC Trustee Midwestern Baptist Theological Seminary (Chairman of the Board of Trustees one year) Trustee Lifeway- SBC

Mission trips: Botswana, South Africa, Australia, Philippines

If the Birth of Christ is
in This Generation

*(What is the Perspective of this
Present World System?)*

If the birth of Christ is happening today, I'm very much sure there will be mixed emotions, mixed attitudes and outcome, and mixed belief about His birth. The broadcast coverage in different radio stations, television studios and newspapers may have variety of outlook and reporting. The media will be on hype and will broadcast live via satellite from Jerusalem in spite of the nonstop conflict between countries in the Middle East. The internet will be filled with comments, videos of the Nativity, and there will be selfies with Joseph, Mary and Jesus. And for sure, there will be some disgusting and foolish talk on the part of the atheists. The Facebook status of many regarding the virgin birth will be overwhelmingly filled with share and links of people's opinion. Many will worship the event rather than the Savior. People will be more concern of the technology, the science and political correctness of Christ's birth, and medical answers instead of focusing on the fulfillment of the prophecies, the miracles and the touch of God on Christmas. And the truth of the Word of God might even be disregarded and discard. God has a set time and purpose, and it was a perfect time, with a glorious purpose! But it's not about the timing, but about the atonement and the filled praise birth of a Savior and King.

The kingdoms, the thrones, the seat of powers, and the political arena will be filled with jealousy, insecurities and envies. It will be rocked by the Rock of Ages- the Lord and Savior of the whole world. He is the "Only One" as the song says; "He is the Only One, the One that can save you, He is the Only hope, the Only One that can do, all you gotta do is admit you're a sinner, repent from your sins, then become a believer…" (From the Album: "Ten Thousand Years" CD by Eliezer Dumala Sagansay. John said: "9- The next day John seeth Jesus coming unto him, and saith, Behold the Lamb of God, which taketh away the sin of the world. 30- This is he of whom I said, After me cometh a man which is preferred before me: for he was before me." (John 1:29- 30 KJV) He will not only take away our sins; but He will be worship and every nations and tongues will bow down before Him to honor Him as King of kings and Lord of lords! Apostle Paul wrote; "5- Let this mind be in you, which was also in Christ Jesus: 6- Who, being in the form of God, thought it not robbery to be equal with God: 7- But made himself of no reputation, and took upon him the form of a servant, and was made in the likeness of men: 8- And being found in fashion as a man, he humbled himself, and became obedient unto death, even the death of the cross. 9- Wherefore God also hath highly exalted him, and given him a name which is above every name: 10- That at the name of Jesus every knee should bow, of things in heaven, and things in earth, and things under the earth; 11- And that every tongue should confess that Jesus Christ is Lord, to the glory of God the Father." (Philippians 2:5- 11 King James Version)

What would the present day kings and presidents say to Jesus, Mary and Joseph if the fulfillment of the prophecies occurs in this troubled generation? It can be different from Herod's words and perspective but the same purpose and agenda. It will be political, selfish, destructive, and ungodly attitude! At the end of the day, everyone will be standing before the throne of God for judgment. It means as it's obviously true that thrones are a seats of authority and power. It means that no matter how powerful, wealthy, and respected we are; we will all bow down to the newborn King- the Lord Jesus Christ! At the end of the ages, no one will remain in power but the One and only powerful, the child in a manger. This is not just a fact but the truth based in the Word of God. He was born an ordinary baby, from an ordinary mother with an ordinary foster father appointed by God the Father. And this extra ordinary man named Joseph was not aware beforehand what God has in stored for him. Let us know some of the Josephs in the Bible so we will have the definite idea of who we are giving due and tribute as, or if needed be given to the greatest foster father in the world.

Josephs in the Bible

There are a few *Josephs* mentioned in the scriptures. In the book of Genesis; Joseph the son of Jacob and Rachel was born while Jacob was serving his uncle Laban. (Genesis 30:22- 25) Joseph was beloved of his father Jacob. Joseph of Arimathaea is the unpopular one. We are going to learn from Joseph the husband of Mary, beloved of God the Father. God the Father chose him to be the foster father of Jesus. Like Joseph the son of Jacob, he went through a lot too. Children blame their parents or their past for not being a good father to their children or vice versa. Notice here the man who was brought up in a complicated home, a broken family, and "play favorites" parents. Let us unfold the summary of the life of Joseph, the son of Jacob:

Joseph of the Old Testament
(Genesis 30:22- 26)

Leah's 2 great news before Joseph's birth could be the turning point in her life. It was when God looked back and remember her, and said; "a child would be born". But the great news along with it was when the Bible says; "And

God remembered Rachel, *and God hearken to her,* and opened her womb." Joseph was born after God turned His mind and His face to Rachel. For me, those were powerful words and very encouraging words for a woman who was going through a lot. Those are encouraging words for all of us whether we are in the valley or in a mountain top experience. Rachel and Joseph knew what it meant to be in those unpleasant experiences, as well as great and prosperous life. But God has a purpose as what Joseph said later in his life. (Genesis 50:19- 20)

Joseph's Childhood (Genesis 30:22- 27; 37:1- 20)

- Joseph witnessed the hardships and the conflict between Jacob his father and Laban his uncle.
- Joseph heard about the news when his sister Dinah was defiled by Shechem the Hivite. (Genesis 34:1- 5)
- Joseph witnessed how his brothers deceived the family of Shechem and killed them. (Genesis 34:6- 31)

Joseph's Life as a Youth (Genesis Chapters 38 to 39)

- Joseph was an ordinary shepherd. (Genesis 37:2)
- Joseph witnessed his father Jacob's conflict with his wife, and he witnessed Jacob playing favorites among his children. (Genesis 37:1- 14)
- Joseph was envied, hated and sold by his brothers. (Genesis 37:15- 36)

Ely R. S.

- Joseph was tempted and was put in prison. (Genesis 39:1- 23)
- Joseph was betrayed by a friend (Genesis 40:23)

Joseph's Life in Egypt as Prime Minister (Genesis 45:8 to chapter 50)

Joseph became so powerful in the kingdom and he was the key to its prosperity and success. We know the power and respect he gained as the new prime minister of Egypt. He was reconciled to his brethren and he got the retribution in a godly manner. The good report about Joseph made the neighboring countries stand in awe of how he governed the nation in spite of poverty, famine, and hardships in the lives of his people. He made a great exodus from the impending downfall by the wisdom, power, and revelation of God through his dream. He then made an exemplary move by the guidance of the Holy Spirit as King Pharaoh gave him all the authority and power.

Joseph of Arimathaea (John 19:37- 42)

In the book of John, we have here Joseph of Arimathaea. He may not be an expert of the Word, but he was a man with a generous heart, and a man who was willing to stand before Pilate on behalf of the disciples. He risked his life so Jesus would have a decent burial and decent tomb. The Bible called him "the honorable counselor, who waited for the Kingdom of God". (Mark 15:43- 46) In the scriptures, he was actually called a good and just man. "And, behold, there was a man named Joseph, a counsellor; and he was a good man, and a just." (Luke 23:50 KJV)

Joseph of Arimathaea was the Secret Agent as a Christian

I agree Joseph of Arimathaea was the secret agent in the burial of Jesus. (Matthew 27:57- 60) Joseph of Arimathaea was the secret agent for the disciples. Joseph of Arimathaea was influential and rich. He was a man of honor and integrity. The Bible says; "(The same had not consented to the counsel and deed of them) he was of Arimathaea, a city of the Jews: who also himself waited for the kingdom of God." (Luke 23:51 KJV)

Joseph the Foster Father of Jesus in the Flesh

- He was a faithful Christian who loved Mary.
- He was a chosen man of God.
- He was willing to sacrifice for God.
- He was a courageous man of God.
- He was called to take the responsibility and the duty to serve.
- He was a man of honor and integrity.
- He loved the Lord, and he was willing to obey God's Word and God's will.
- He was not selfish, self-centered, proud or arrogant. Joseph was a man of God and a man for God.
- He was a man of the Word and for the Word.
- He was a family man, and he loved his family.

Joseph loved God. We must love our family because God loves our family more than we do. He cares for every single family circle in every corner of the globe. They all went through the same struggles in life and the same problems, but God knows what's best for Joseph and what's best for you.

"Was it 21 Days to Christmas, Joseph?"

"And she shall bring forth a son, and thou shalt call his name JESUS: for he shall save his people from their sins." (Matthew 1:21 KJV)

I was privileged to preach a Christmas message in a Christmas cantata with this topic: "Christmas: 1 to 21 Days" and my text was taken from Matthew 1:21. The message was in relation to what would you do from 1 to 21 days before Christmas if you were Joseph? Mary's message to Joseph could be: "Its 21 days before the first Christmas, Joseph!"

> You rush through the traffic and that's really terrific,
> You work hard to save some money on
> Christmas day to give away;
> I don't mean to be rude, but the Christian's right attitude,
> Twenty one days before Christmas…
> it is to worship God with gratitude

What would be the best thing you could do 21 days before Christmas? Or what can you do for God, for your family, or for your church and ministry 21 (or fewer days) before Christmas? Would you be willing to give your life and your all to Jesus? The Bible said; "Glory to God in the highest, and on earth peace, goodwill toward men." (Luke 2:14 KJV) It's a message of peace, goodwill, and salvation for all men. God is interested in us and our salvation, and that's the reason why He sent us His only begotten Son. We must remember that the Lord is more interested in us than in our past. He paid for it at the cross of Calvary and shed His blood for our sins. Make your first Christmas day with Christ as a new believer count because He is worthy of our praise.

> It doesn't matter if it's your first true Christmas day,
> As a believer, we know it's different from the past;
> What matters most is that your life you will lay…
> In God's throne and in God's hand and
> in His will, we will trust and obey

Joseph and Mary in a Roller Coaster Ride

> "And Joseph also went up from Galilee, out of the
> city of Nazareth, into Judaea, unto the city of David,
> which is called Bethlehem; (because he was of the
> house and lineage of David)." (Luke 2:4 KJV)

Notice the stages of Joseph's emotions from the time he was engaged to Mary up to the time where they have to leave Bethlehem. In verse eighteen it says; "When as his mother Mary was espoused to Joseph, before they came together…"

1) Was it joy and the excitement of Joseph being engaged to Mary or fear and resentment? The Bible was silent about Joseph's attitude towards Mary when he found

out she was pregnant, but one thing is for sure- he was afraid. It's obvious in Matthew 1:19 that Joseph was hesitant to make the relationship public, as well as Mary's pregnancy. Matthew Henry wrote: "Here we have…Mary's espousal to Joseph. Mary, the mother of our Lord, *was espoused to Joseph,* not completely married, but contracted; a purpose of marriage solemnly declared in words *de futuro—that regarding the future,* and a promise of it made if God permit. We read of a man who *has betrothed a wife and has not taken her,* Deu. 20:7. Christ was born of a virgin, but a betrothed virgin: 1. To put respect upon the marriage state, and to recommend it *as honourable among all,* against that doctrine of devils which *forbids to marry,* and places perfection in the single state. Who more highly favored than Mary was in her espousals? 2. To save the credit of the blessed virgin, which otherwise would have been exposed. It was fit that her conception should be protected by a marriage, and so justified in the eye of the world. One of the ancients says, "It was better it should be asked, 'is not this the *son of a carpenter?'* than, 'is not this the *son of a harlot?"*(The Bible Collection)

2) And then the gear had to shift to something that was new and unknown to Joseph; he was told that Mary *"was found with child of the Holy Ghost."* It's common for men to be informed by their wives or OB/GYN specialists (obstetrics and gynecology) about the pregnancy. By the way, *OB/GYN specialists (obstetrics and gynecology, often abbreviated to, OBG, O&G or Obs & Gyno) are the two* surgical– *medical specialties dealing with the female*

reproductive organs in their pregnant *and* non-pregnant state". *(Wikipedia-Yahoo.com)*

But in this case, to be informed by an angel of the Lord regarding your wife's pregnancy is another story. And the message or the announcement of the pregnancy, and how she got pregnant was not ordinary or common. Every single thing that happened before and after the birth of the Lord Jesus Christ was under the control of the Holy Trinity. The OB/GYN don't have the answer unto how she got pregnant.

Joseph's gear shifting, which was beyond his control could be stressful on his part. Joseph who was informed by an angel of the Lord is completely a different story as opposite if informed by Mary herself or by the OB/GYN. Mary may have had problems explaining her pregnancy to her parents, to Joseph, and her friends. It was hard for Joseph to accept Mary's pregnancy which was against the law and could cost Mary her life. She could be stoned to death as according to the Old Testament law. (John 8:1-11) Even if they've been betrothed, they still have to remain pure for a year before they can be together. Life for Mary and Joseph would never be the same. It was a shift in their lives filled with gossip, fear, and maybe worse than we could imagine. It was a struggle, the kind of trials and afflictions and problems that Christians will never go through even during and after the times of Joseph. Their lives were filled with miracles and unanswered questions. During their times, they didn't have the comfort of medical clinics and the comfort of having doctors and nurses by your side. I was thinking of God having a good sense of humor. He used Joseph to be Mary's husband and became a father to Jesus who was mature spiritually, loving, and a good OB/ GYN which means a midwife to his wife Mary. Back then, they don't have instant milk, the disposable diapers, good bottled and clean water.

The comfort of lying in a soft and comfortable bed while giving birth would be next to impossible. It would be a natural feeling for Joseph to be uncomfortable, embarrassed, disappointed, sad, or feeling sorry for Mary delivering a baby in a manger. But the biggest deal for Joseph could be the confession of Mary being pregnant. The angel of the Lord was the one who announced the "good news" about the pregnancy of Mary. It was "good news" for God, the angel of the Lord, and for us; but not for Joseph and Mary at that time- it was a mixed emotion for the couple. It ushers them into a very questionable life, and becoming a bad public example. Their testimony and Christian life were ushered into a *huge* question mark.

Joseph's big questions of the day could be: "How in the world did she get pregnant? How did it happen? And what do you mean of "she was found with child of the Holy Ghost ... and for that which is conceived in her is of the Holy Ghost." It's something that even a medical doctor, an expert in theology, or someone with the Ph.D. or an expert in science or biology could never understand or comprehend. And of course, we discovered the truth when we have the findings in the Scriptures and commentaries, as well as the revelation of the Holy Spirit. The common term for this generation is "weird". The advanced technology of our time will not have an answer and cannot answer such miracle. It shows us of the hand of God on Mary's womb. King David in the book of Psalm said: "For thou hast possessed my reins: thou hast covered me in my mother's womb. 14- I will praise thee; for I am fearfully and wonderfully made: marvelous are thy works; and that my soul knoweth right well. 15- My substance was not hid from thee, when I was made in secret, and curiously wrought in the lowest parts of the earth. 16- Thine eyes did see my substance, yet being unperfect; and in thy book all my members were written, which in continuance were fashioned, when as yet there was none of them." (Psalm 139:13- 116 KJV)

It was just fine for King David and for us to say such words, because we have the scriptures. Of course it is a miracle, but David has a biological father which was different from the Lord Jesus Christ who was born by the Holy Ghost. Mary's conception of the Savior and the Lord's birth was God's intervention, and the Father's miraculous hand working in her life and in her womb. This could be the same question in the minds of millions of people: "How in the world did she get pregnant and how did it happen?"

3) "Then Joseph her husband, being a just man, and not willing to make her a public example, was minded to put her away privily." (Matthew 1:19 KJV) You can feel the emotional and mental torture that Joseph went through in the midst of what God had bid him do. Of course, Mary may have the same feelings, but it would not be as much questions as what Joseph may have had in his sound mind. We know that he was doing the will of God; but that does not spare him from the emotional pain, and the ridicule of the people. Praise God for those who will play the role of Joseph in a Christmas cantata or Christmas play, but I believe you can play the role of Joseph better if you will think of his actual condition and situations on that day.

We just started the roller coaster ride with Joseph and Mary as the main drivers, but God was the one who controlled the wheels. Joseph's pain made him step up to prosperity and greater blessings. Their struggles took them to success and God's blessings. Joseph's sacrifices took him to the greatest history and event, and now an occasion which the whole world celebrates with joy, peace, and gift giving generation after generations.

Joseph was humbled by the Lord through the responsibilities God had placed on his shoulders. I personally believe that God would not have allowed Joseph to take responsibilities that were beyond his capability and strength. And God would not let Mary carry something that was beyond her strength, and beyond what she could carry in her heart and mind. God knows our mind, our hearts, our weakness, and our whole being.

> You may be small and nothing less…
> But Christ has plan for you to rest,
> You tried and failed and on your knees
> He'll lift you up to give you success.

> "Which were born, not of blood, nor of
> the will of the flesh, nor of the will of
> man, but of God." (John 1:13 KJV)

The Crescendo in Joseph's Life

"And Jacob begat Joseph the husband of Mary, of whom was born Jesus, who is called Christ." (Matthew 1:16 KJV)

What happened to Mary and Joseph was absolutely the hand of God, and we cannot argue about it. It's the truth, it was the will of God, it was factual, and we have the records from the Word of God.

> "Crescendo" means cres·cen·dos or cres·cen·di (-d)
> 1. Abbr. cr. Music
> a. A gradual increase, especially in the volume
> or intensity of sound in a passage.
> b. A passage played with a gradual
> increase in volume or intensity.
> 2. a. A steady increase in intensity or force: "insisted [that]
> all paragraphs … should be structured as a crescendo
> rising to a climactic last sentence" (Henry A. Kissinger)

b. Usage Problem. The climactic point or moment after such a progression: (The Free Dictionary on Yahoo)

What are the climactic points in Joseph's life? What are the climactic points in Joseph's life before and after Christmas? The moment when Mary talked to him about her pregnancy? Was it when everyone knows about Mary's pregnancy which could cost him his life and Mary's life? Was it when Joseph and Mary was the bullet of all the gossips that the people were trying to shoot at every day? Or it could be the appearance and the announcement of the angels about God's purpose and plan? If Joseph was not a mature, godly, loving, and dedicated servant of God; I don't think he would have made it to the end of the Christmas action and drama. Abraham, Isaac and Jacob had their own series of events in their lifetime. Even Samson had his own love story, suspenseful stages of unforgettable events, and circumstances with action and drama. Samson went into the doors and ladders of surprises from the Philistines, the devil and from the Lord. Everyone has their own music in life wherein you either have to sing, dance, or slow down at times. You would need to shout for joy or remorse for days, hours, or even years. Some people can't overcome their resentment, bitterness, hatred, and failures in their heart in which many have brought down their life to the bottom.

The word "crescendo" is unfamiliar, foreign, and a questionable word for them. You can be comfortable at the bottom, play a stagnant and a monotone lifestyle, or take your life to a crescendo of blessings and prosperity with the Lord. In spite of challenges, struggles, and disadvantages in life; stay focus and keep on climbing the ladder to success. Take that climactic climb with the Lord, and don't be dismayed by what other people will say or may say to you and about you! If Joshua and Moses were there; they will give Joseph and Mary the same advice as what they have heard from God during their tough times, God said; "5- There shall not any man be able to stand before thee all the days of thy life: as I was with Moses, so I will be with thee: I will not fail thee, nor forsake thee. 6- Be strong and of a good courage: for unto this people shalt thou divide for an inheritance the land, which I sware unto their fathers to give them. 7- Only be thou strong and very courageous, that thou mayest observe to do according to all the law, which Moses my servant commanded thee: turn not from it to the right hand or to the left, that thou mayest prosper whithersoever thou goest. (Joshua 1:5- 7 KJV)

Tough Decisions are Part of the Crescendo's in Life

I was wondering about the decision of Joseph regarding the pregnancy of Mary. What if Joseph backed off, and did not take the challenge, the blessing, and the opportunity and responsibility of being a husband to Mary. The greatest responsibility and duty that God the Father has offered to men was to be a foster father to Jesus. And Joseph got the job or ministry. If Joseph failed God on this offer, he may have had a miserable life. Joseph may have missed the blessings of God. Joseph may have missed the peace, the joy, and the touch of God in his life. It was if he refused the offer of God through His angel. My personal view of taking Mary as Joseph's wife which is against the Jewish law because they were not married was something that only the grace of God could make him take the challenge.

Let's think of the opposite regarding Joseph's right attitude toward God, His word and His will. God's plan was for Mary to be with child. And what do you think Joseph would do? He wanted to dump Mary because he doesn't want his testimony to be ruined by Mary's early pregnancy. What if he decided to go the other way? What would be Joseph's life and future after his conversations with the angel of God? Joseph may have end up as a plain carpenter. He would not be a blessing from his generation unto the end of generations. He would be miserable in his lifetime. Mary would not be his wife. He may have lost the greatest responsibility, duty and blessings of being a part of the greatest event in the history of mankind- the birth of the Lord Jesus Christ. We would not be hearing and reading the name "Joseph" on every Christmas story and play.

Should Joseph fail God on this offer; he would not go any higher in his roller coaster ride in his whole lifetime. He would never know how to have a Christian life in crescendo to God's plan and purpose for mankind. Joseph would never have any idea of what it means to be up on the peak of the mountain of blessings with God on your side. He took the challenge of the angel, and the ministry of God to minister to Jesus and to the generations to come. It was from the lowest notes to the highest notes in his life, and Joseph remained faithful to God. He was *down-beat* and *bit up* but not *fed up* and he *went up* with his *hands up* for God. Mister

Steve Green has a song entitled "Symphony of Praise." The beautiful message of the song ministered to millions of people. The Songwriters are Dennis, John Randall / Mohr, Jon. I can picture God as the conductor of the universe, and He is in control of everything.

It's a very powerful song with a powerful message. If Joseph's life was a hymn of praise or a music piece, how would it sound? How would you picture the ups and downs of the music? Imagine how God would strike a note, and use His baton to lead Joseph's life to its highest crescendo and then drop it in a split of a second. I will never understand the feeling of falling and falling, not knowing what would happen next. God let Joseph fall down on his knees, and humbled him because God wants to do greater things in him and through him. Sometimes God will bring us to our knees by giving us sickness, sufferings, and even success in life to bring us down to our knees. The announcement of the angel was a message from God that could turn his life upside down and it did. This was a turning point of his life that will break him and make him the father of Jesus in the flesh.

I remember coming to the office of Dr. Gavino S. Tica. Pastor Tica was the president of our mission board in the Philippines. He is a man of God that I respect and love so dearly. I can't forget the night I came to Dr. Tica's office and discussed to him about my desire to work overseas. I confided to Dr. Tica about my desire and burden to do mission work in North America. And to be definite; he asked me where in America. I told him, "Doctor Tica, anywhere in the United States of America, and wherever God will lead us there." Doctor Tica said: "That's the joke of the century, Ely…" He shared to me the struggles, the problems, and lack of financial support of the pastors, and missionaries that were already in the States. At the end of our conversations and I could never forget what he said, "Ely, working in the USA as a pastor or missionary will either make you or break you."

Our circumstances, our trials, the opportunities that we have in the Lord will either break us or make us. It depends on your attitude or your perspective, and on how you see things. It may also depend on your love, faith, and relationship with God. What is your attitude while you're on the top of your roller coaster rides? Have you seen yourself at the bottom, and been humbled by the Lord as you looked down from the top as the Lord leads you to a roller coaster ride? Did you see yourself as an instrument or a main player? Did you see yourself in God's hand, or did you see the big "I", "ME", and "MY" in your stairway to success?

Everything that went on in Joseph and Mary's life could lead them to a big "question mark" as they looked at it as either good news or bad news. It depends on how you look at the God-given opportunity, and how to deal with the issues. Your sincere love and faith to God will play a big role. If you love the Lord and your faith is strong; all other issues will just be *"another issue in life"*. The needs, the future, the struggles, and road blocks will just be a vital part of your crescendo to God's will and greater purpose in life. Remember *God's Will* is greater than what people perceive and would think of it. God's permissive will excel above human's negative reactions towards Joseph and Mary. "God's will" must excel over man's will. It must be on the center of our life, our home, in our churches and job or business.

Joseph could identify himself with those who didn't see the future due to the blackness of the clouds of God. Joseph made a steady walk through the black clouds of God, knowing that God was on the other side of the clouds waiting for him. If I could only picture in my limited mind how Mary and Joseph talked about their life, from their boyfriend/girlfriend relationship up to the time when Mary was beneath the cross of Christ at Calvary. I cannot imagine the grief, and the mixed emotions with joy and peace. If you think of Mary as she looked at her womb, from day one until the day she delivers the baby Jesus. And then she would look at Jesus in a dirty, smelly manger of Bethlehem with the singing and worshipping animals around them. The noise of the animals in that little room, the mowing or the crying of the sheep became music to Jesus' ears.

She watched Him grow from a little child to a young man. They watched Him as He taught the doctors and the Pharisees of the truth of the Word of God. He also preached in the busy streets of Jerusalem and in the synagogue. And one of the greatest memories Mary may recall was when she watched Him perform miracles. They witnessed how Jesus multiplied the bread and healed the sick. The pain was there when Mary was at the foot of the cross when the Lord was bleeding and was in intense pain. The sorrow and the pain were mixed by the hope and the joy that God had promised through Him. Some Bible scholars believe that Joseph died before Jesus was crucified. If this was true, then it could have been harder for Mary.

If Mary could share something to Joseph about their life from the announcement of the angel until the resurrection, she may have said: "The last time I touched the blood was my own blood in the body of our baby Jesus. When I was at the cross while Jesus was bleeding for our sins, the blood that touched my body was His own blood that dropped for every human being, from this day until the last man or woman who will come to know Him as Savior and Lord." The blood is for everyone until the end of the world. The event at the cross of Calvary was the lowest point in Mary's life; but it was the greatest victory from God for sinful men! And it was the greatest defeat in human history. It was a defeat of the powerful evil in principalities and power! It was the fulfillment of what God had promised through His angel, the destruction of our enemy- sin and Satan. Our lowest point does not mean failure or it's the end. We may be at the end of our rope, but God has an extended rope with a blessed hope in Jesus.

Imagine the feelings of those who received a letter from their organization or company, from their church or mission board with the indication of either losing support or losing a job. I was in the same situation a few years ago, and it was so discouraging and I was devastated. I remember those who died in Mindanao, in the Southern part of the Philippines and those who died in the Yolanda tragedy in Tacloban,

Philippines. Thousands were suffering and were declared dead from the flash flood. I know it's hard to reconcile the discouraging news in your life, and the devastation in many parts of the world right now as compared to what the angels said on that first Christmas day. The Bible says; "And the angel said unto them, Fear not: for, behold, I bring you good tidings of great joy, which shall be to all people. 14- Glory to God in the highest, and on earth peace, good will toward men." (Luke 2:10; 14 KJV) "And they shall call his name Emmanuel, which being interpreted is, God with us." (Matthew 1:23 KJV) God will be with us and He will help us.

Life is tough and the road is rough,
But we can cling to the angel's announcements,
About God's perfect plan,
He knows the past, present and the future;
So why be discouraged when God is in control.

"Way to Go... Joseph!"

You made it in your first round Joseph, but you have more rounds to go. I love to watch boxing, and I like boxers who are aggressive and determined to fight and hit their opponent. The first two rounds are kind of boring sometimes, because both boxers are feeling and studying their opponent's style and moves. After two rounds, it will still be, "Way to go... for both boxers," unless there is a knockout. Who wants to get knocked down or knocked out on our way to win or as we strive to reach our goals? Mary's pregnancy by the Holy Ghost was just the first round of what God had in store for Joseph. It means "way to go… Joseph!" It is hard to determine if Joseph will make it if you study the series of events in Joseph's life… and indeed the conclusion is: "Way to go… Joseph!"

In the book of Matthew it says; "And when they were departed, behold, the angel of the Lord appeareth to Joseph in a dream, saying, 'Arise, and take the young child and his mother, and flee into Egypt, and be thou there until I bring thee word: for Herod will seek the young child to destroy him." (Matthew 2:13 KJV) They just rested for a while when they travelled to pay their taxes. The Scripture says; "1- And it came to pass in those days, that there went out a decree from Caesar Augustus that all the world should be taxed. 2- (And this taxing was first made when Cyrenius was governor of Syria.) 3- And all went to be taxed, every one into his own city. 4- And Joseph also went up from Galilee, out of the city of Nazareth, into Judaea, unto the city of David, which is called Bethlehem; (because he was of the house and lineage of David:)" (Luke 2:1- 4 KJV) After the birth of Jesus as stated in the book of Matthew chapter two verses twelve to eighteen that they have to arise, leave, and go to Egypt to hide from the wrath of king Herod. I could not imagine the fear, the stress in the life of Joseph and Mary after the announcement of the angel. If I will make a new word for their experiences with the angels; I will call it "Angelicnewsphobia". Every time they get news from the angel, it was not always pleasant, and it will scare you to death to receive such news. It requires a lot of faith and grace.

In His conversations with His disciples, and to the people around Him in a village of the Samaritans, Jesus said: "Foxes have holes, and birds of the air have nests; but the Son of man hath not where to lay his head." (Luke 9:58 KJV) From the time Mary was pregnant up to her due date; Mary, Joseph, and Jesus were homeless. We have the Nativity and all the pictures that you may have seen since childhood. The Nativity scene is obviously not an actual place, but the truth of what the Bible was saying about Jesus being in a manger cannot be denied. It could be worse, or beyond our imagination of which the greatest painter and artists could not even paint it in a canvas without an emotion or tears from their eyes. The Bible says: "And she brought forth her firstborn son, and wrapped him in swaddling clothes, and laid him in a manger; because there was no room for them in the inn." (Luke 2:7 KJV) As much as the people during Jesus' time had "no room for them in the inn" in terms of physical room that they could offer to them so they could spend a night under a roof. People in such times as these refused to let Jesus come into their hearts. Jesus wants to come *into* our hearts, so He can sit on the throne of our hearts. He wants to come in not for convenience, protection, or shelter; Jesus wants to come in to have a love relationship with us. Our hearts is similar or worse when compared to the *inn* that was offered to Mary and Joseph. Our hearts are defiled, dirty, sinful, and blackened by sin and disgrace. (Mark 7:21- 23) Jesus, the holy Son of God wants to come in and dwell in our hearts. He wants to clean our hearts by the blood that He shed on the cross more than 2,000 years ago.

Joseph Made a Positive Impact in His Family and Community

Notice the response of Joseph as the Lord tested his knowledge, his wisdom, and the depths of his love and his conviction for the Word of God.

- Joseph was obedient and positive. (Matthew 1:18-19 and 2:13- 14)
- Joseph did not let fear control him, and he was not overcome by fear. (Matthew 1:20; II Timothy 1:7)
- Joseph listened and obeyed the angels of God. (Matthew 1:20- 25; 2:13- 14)
- Joseph exercised his self-control in spite of the struggles, problems, criticism and trials in life. (Matthew 2:14; 21)
- Joseph took the steps of faith from the time he took Mary until the time where they have to flee into Egypt to escape from Herod's deadly and vicious wrath. (Matthew 2:13-15)
- Joseph was never mentioned in the Bible to identify him with sin, failure, or submission to temptation.
- Joseph lived a holy life in spite of worldly distractions. If I was in Joseph's shoes, I would be overwhelmed with the responsibilities and the instant changes of events in my life.

Joseph learned to walk the talk.
He took the step of faith although his life was at stake.
He followed the Savior 'till he was distraught.
He was an example for us to follow
in His love we will walk…

It Was a Rough Road for Joseph and Mary

"But when Herod was dead, behold, an angel of the Lord appeareth in a dream to Joseph in Egypt, 20- Saying, Arise, and take the young child and his mother, and go into the land of Israel: for they are dead which sought the young child's life." (Matthew 2:19- 20 KJV)

Literally, Joseph and Mary walked through rough roads. When Joseph and Mary decided to travel from Nazareth to Bethlehem; they also had to consider their safety, food and other necessities, as well as the distance, the rain, the heat of the sun, and desert storms. It was also the issues of discomfort and inconvenience. The comfort of the bright star and the joy of service in their hearts were treasures from God. The star was a sign, a bright light of hope, of peace and of joy. The star was the good news of salvation that made Joseph, Mary, the wise men, and the shepherds "keep going" in spite of the rough roads in life. For King Herod; it could mean losing a kingdom, his power, and his wealth. It could be the star of fear for him because of his selfishness and greediness. Jesus was not born to take the kingdom from Herod, He gave it to him. He did not come to take the kingdom from man, but He came to give us the kingdom of heaven. (John 3:1- 7)

It's so sad that while some of the politicians are worried about politics, millions of people suffered because of their greediness and selfishness. King Herod and Caesar Augustus worried about their next term, while their people suffered in their terms and under their godless terms. Notice what Matthew 1:19 says, "And not willing to make her a public example, was minded to put her away privily." I assumed that Mary and Joseph may have had a little discussion, and may have an argument over Joseph's idea of *putting her away* due to her early pregnancy. Mary at those times was very young. Some scholars have said that Mary was about 12 to 15 years of age. In verse 20: "But while he thought on these things…" It was not an easy road for Joseph; it was so hard for him and Mary that the Bible through the working of the Holy Spirit had it mentioned in Matthew 1:20. It was something to think about as they were together doing the will of the Father.

Notice the preceding phrase in verse 20: "Fear not to take unto thee Mary thy wife." Then came the spiritual struggle of Joseph. We may have read this over and over every Christmas day, but for Joseph it was a different story and perspective. The angel made an announcement to Joseph; "And she shall bring forth a son, and thou shalt call his name JESUS: for he shall save his people from their sins." It means that God had chosen him (Joseph) to stand as a father of Jesus, and God was entrusting to Joseph the physical, emotional, and the spiritual upbringing of the Savior of the world. As my African- American friend would jokingly say to me with an accent: "It is weird Ely, ain't it?" Then they have moved and exercise their duty by paying their taxes.

They travelled from Nazareth to Bethlehem to pay their taxes in spite of her pregnancy. (Luke 2:1- 5 KJV)

Mary may have been eight to nine months pregnant. It was not fun at all travelling with just a donkey or a camel in a desert place and rough roads. God used the decree from Caesar Augustus on taxing to fulfill His promise. Jesus would indeed be born in Bethlehem as promised. Micah prophesied; "But thou, Bethlehem Ephratah, though thou be little among the thousands of Judah, yet out of thee shall he come forth unto me that is to be ruler in Israel; whose goings forth have been from of old, from everlasting. 3- Therefore will he give them up, until the time that she which travaileth hath brought forth: then the remnant of his brethren shall return unto the children of Israel." (Micah 5:2- 3 KJV)

God will not always make us walk on a shiny marble or on a plain path, but we can be sure of the fact that God will be with us if the road is rough. They climbed every mountain, crossed every river and pond, journeyed through the hills, and walked through the valley of the shadows of death with the assurance that God was with them as they took part in God's plan. It was a testimony of God's grace that they were able to make it in Bethlehem. But with all the ups and down in life and down the road to God's perfect will; Mary gave birth to a healthy baby. It was a blessed day for Mary and Joseph because not only that Jesus was born, but because they know they did the perfect will of God in their lives. "Glory to God in the Highest…"

I wonder what kind of people the owners of the manger were; but one thing for sure, at least they offered an option for Mary and Joseph. Although he or she was better than those who slammed their doors in the face of Mary and Joseph by not letting them stay overnight; the owner of the manger was not their best for Jesus. But at least they have a room for Jesus during that painful night for Mary. It was not easy for Joseph and Mary, the shepherds, and the wise men to follow the bright star of God and to obey the will of God. The song of Marvin Gaye and Tammi Terrell has a beautiful message. Indeed there's no mountain too high for the Lord, and there's no valley and underground river or cave too low for Jesus. He went into the deepest hell after He rose from the dead. For those who are striving, struggling, and walking into a semilar situations as Mary and Joseph; everything that you're going through are just temporary.

There may be mountains and valleys, but if you have Jesus who walks with you, it cannot be higher than God. It cannot be lower than His hand willing to reach out to the lowest of men. Some people on the other side of the world may have celebrated their last Christmas together, after which; was a divorce, or maybe death came in the family. I understand that there will be broken homes celebrating Christmas without mom, without dad, without unity at home, but the worst is without God at home. They celebrate Christmas with so much food and drink on the table, but God is out of the table. You'll never know what it means to have an empty table on Christmas Day until you've been there yourself. You may be on a rough road of life this Christmas, but always remember God is with us and He will help us as we walk through the trials and problems in life. It's an honor, a great privilege, an opportunity to serve; but it comes with a great responsibility. And Joseph has to take the responsibilities. He was expected to keep his testimony and his momentum.

- He has to take good care of Mary, and Mary's pregnancy.
- He has to keep Mary from harm and the evil devices of the devil and his angels.
- Joseph has to protect Mary from Herod and his evil soldiers.
- Joseph has to obey and live the Word of God.
- Joseph must be sensitive to the voice of the Holy Spirit.
- Joseph has to take good care of Jesus and be a good example to Him.

Don't focus on the responsibility as you follow His way,
You just need to be faithful in His Word to obey;
The God who calls you in His field…
In Him you trust and obey,
As the Lord opens the door of opportunity for you.

Joseph Remained Focused on God's Special Day!

I was reading over and over the Christmas story from the books of Matthew and Luke, and I never read a single dialogue on Joseph's part. We have the treasures and the pressure of Christmas, but did you know that Christmas is a treasure from the Lord because of the gift of God the

Father to a dying and sinful world? (Romans 6:23) It will be pressure if you don't know the true meaning, the true spirit and the center of Christmas. People from different backgrounds, cultures, religions, and beliefs have different ways of celebrating Christmas. You may have your own meaning, or practice, and way of celebrating Christmas, but the focus must be the same. You've seen and heard of people who gave their own opinion about Christmas.

If Joseph was not spiritually mature and if he was not living the Christian life; he could never have made it on that first Christmas day. Joseph would be proud and begin to have a haughty spirit, or he would be so scared and turned his back from the offer and command of God through the angel. Some of the people you know may not make it right this Christmas season. It's because they don't know the right person of Christmas which is the Lord Jesus Christ. Remember that Christmas is not about you and it's not about us, it's about the Christ of Christmas. The Bible says; "And she shall bring forth a son, and thou shalt call his name JESUS: for he shall save his people from their sin." (Matthew 1:21 KJV)

The world may focus their hearts and mind to gifts, Santa Claus, celebrations; but the most important thing is to focus our hearts, and worship to God and the Lord Jesus Christ. It's His birthday and the Lord's fulfillment of His prophecy. It is about God's salvation for sinners. Distractions can lead to destructions. You will miss the point and target if you're not focused, especially this Christmas season. We can make Christmas meaningful, and a day to remember by doing something special for our families and friends. We can make it special by being generous to our employers, friends and families. But nothing is more than acceptable, and glorifying to God than having our hearts and our eyes on Jesus. Keep your eyes off from any distractions in this special season, because it might lead you to unexpected destruction!

> It's not the gifts that you shared,
> Can make your Christmas be filled;
> With your love on God's special day
> Remember what matters most to God
> is Christ's salvation for free.

Christians can easily get so distracted with the business, parties, appointments, and Christmas related activities that some may overlook the true spirit of Christmas. The real focus of the season is not the holiday season, but the person- the Lord Jesus Christ. I love the song by Avalon about Christmas that touched millions of lives through its message. The song "We are the Reason" was a big hit. And we all know that we were the reason why Jesus came down to live and die for our sins.

Who and what is your main focus this Christmas? Are you more focused on Christ or on the celebration? Santa Claus, Rudolf, or whoever is taking the spotlight off the Lord's birth is not acceptable to God, not according to what the Bible teaches. We will not let man-made stories and man-made celebrations take over God's special day. It's the birthday of the King. He is worthy of our focus and worship.

The Lord is the center of Christmas,
Be it at church for worship or in a mass
Our focus must not be diverted,
Let us be like Joseph
Who put Jesus in the Center of
Christmas on that special day.

What Was on Joseph's Mind on First Christmas Day?

"And Jacob begat Joseph the husband of Mary, of whom was born Jesus, who is called Christ. 18- Now the birth of Jesus Christ was on this wise: When as his mother Mary was espoused to Joseph, before they came together, she was found with child of the Holy Ghost." (Matthew 1:16; 18 KJV)

You may already know that Joseph was not the father in the flesh of the Lord Jesus Christ, because Jesus Christ was born of a virgin by the working of the Holy Spirit of God. The relationship between Joseph and Mary was active already, although not into the highest extent, as in the husband and wife relationship. The Scriptures says; "When as his mother Mary was espoused to Joseph, before they came together..." The Jewish law requires the couples to be espoused before marriage. They have what they call the formal agreement, or witness agreement between two parties. This is a one-year waiting period or engagement stage. This can only be broken by divorce. The other one would be the ceremony where they will be pronounced as husband and wife.

If I were in Joseph's situation, I definitely would have mixed emotions. I would be emotionally hyped because Jesus would be born in a few months. I would be spiritually anxious because I'm going to serve God the Father through Him. He is the King of kings and the Lord of lords. I could be mentally drained by the time Mary gave birth, because I would be thinking day and night on how I could be a good father and be an example to Jesus. I should be Bible-centered, Biblically right and focused. I also need to obtain God's wisdom, knowledge, and understanding. The need to be filled with the Holy Spirit of God was not an option. All those days, months or weeks were not enough for Joseph to think of so many things and many ways that he can do for them on first Christmas day. So as with those who are celebrating Christmas with the wrong focus, wrong motive, and in a wrong person. What God wants for us to do is for us to submit in His will, and God will take care of the rest.

Sometimes we get excited with the celebration and got out of focus on the Celebrant. But on your countdown to Christmas, what do you have in mind? What is your mind set, perspective, and what or to whom do you focus your attention the most? As you count the days to Christmas day, count on the Savior, because He is the reason for the season!

> I count the gifts and friends on Christmas day,
> To share my time and wealth for free;
> But I forgot it's the Savior's birth,
> And He's the One to celebrate.

Christmas is in the Heart of God

It's your Christmas too!" That was the answer of a boy who was told by a man about the boy's Christmas celebration. The boy responded with his arms open, and so much emotion and said: "It's your Christmas too!" A Sunday school student made a sarcastic remark during their Sunday school question and answer in relation to Christmas and genealogy. The boy said: "Who cares about the genealogy anyways?" It's the prevailing mindset of our generation: "who cares about..." It is logically saying to God that the "genealogy" is not part of the Bible. Matthew wrote; "And Jacob begat Joseph the husband of Mary, of whom was born Jesus, who is called Christ. 17- So all the generations from Abraham to David are fourteen generations; and from David until the carrying away into Babylon are fourteen generations; and from the carrying away into Babylon unto Christ are fourteen generations." (Matthew 1:16- 17 KJV)

The Lord Jesus Christ is the key to the New Testament, and He locked the Old Testament with His birth. It's not just by His birth but His life, His death, burial, and resurrection. What I mean by "He locked the Old Testament with His birth" is He came to fulfill all the prophecies about Him. It means that there will be no more prophecies in addition to Old Testament books after Malachi. It means the Old Testament will start its countdown regarding its prophecies about the Messiah, and its fulfillment unto the end of the age. The New Testament from Christ's genealogy will start pointing to the Old Testament with regards to its prophecies about the Messiah. The New Testament started with Christ and ended with the prophecies of His reign according to the book of Revelation. It would be in the new heaven and new earth. The Bible says; "I am Alpha and Omega, the beginning and the end, the first and the last." (Revelation 22:13 KJV) His genealogy has a special significance in the Bible because it ushered in the Old Testament story, and *His* story from the past to the future. The Old Testament looks forward to His life, His death and His reign as King of kings and Lord of lords. The New Testament looks back to the fulfillment of the prophecies of His birth, and looks forward to His coming upon the rapture of the church.

The Lord Jesus Christ was the one who completed the New Testament, and He is the key to the grace mentioned in the Bible. If they had a background check during His time; the genealogy of Christ is the answer to the background check on the promised Messiah! Jesus was from the lineage of Adam, Abraham, Isaac, Jacob, up to King David…and to Joseph the husband of Mary in the New Testament. You don't need to know every details of the genealogy of Jesus Christ to know Him in a personal way. And for you to have an intimate relationship with Him; you need to invite Him to come into your heart. You need to know Him as your Savior and Lord. (Galatians 4:4- 5)

Christmas is the key to the cross of Calvary. The Old and the New Testament are divided by what Jesus did on Mount Calvary, but both the Old and New Testament look up into it. Christmas will lead you to the cross of Calvary! Jesus humbled Himself and He took your place on the cross, so He could receive you into His place in heaven. But you have to accept Him as your Savior and Lord. You must believe in Him, in His death, burial, and resurrection. Trust in Jesus as the Son of the living God. You may come to the cross in repentance today.

This is a good example of how the Old and New Testament agrees. The Bible was written in different years, from different cultures, different people, different ages, in three languages (Aramaic, Hebrew and Greek) but it does not contradict each other. No wonder the first prophecies from the mouth of God in Genesis 3:15 to the revelation of John from God in the book of Revelation is like a well and perfectly painted story in a canvas.

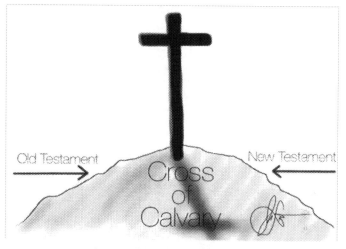

(Artwork by: James Farinas)

It's great to know that salvation is made possible through the Lord Jesus Christ. (John 1:12; 14; 3:16; Ephesians 2:8- 9; Romans 3:10; 23; 6:23; Acts 16:30- 31) He is the center of Christmas and there will be no grace, no salvation without Him.

> Genealogy may don't make sense to thee,
> But as for me, it leads to set me free;
> The Savior who died for me,
> He is the One, and my only Christmas tree.

Christmas opened the door to Christ's death on the cross of Calvary. The cross of Calvary closed the door of the Old Testament laws and ceremonial laws. The burial of Jesus Christ in the tomb opened the door for the burial of sin, and the sting of death with Him for 3 days. Christ's resurrection opened up the grave for the saints and for our salvation. One day, the heaven's gate will open for all His saints during the rapture. (I Corinthians 15:1- 5; I Thessalonians 4:13- 18) Apostle Paul wrote; "And not only so, but we also joy in God through our Lord Jesus Christ, by whom we have now received the atonement." (Romans 5:11 KJV)

The Holy Trinity Planned it All

"For unto us a child is born, unto us a son is given: and the government shall be upon his shoulder: and his name shall be called Wonderful, Counsellor, The mighty God, The everlasting Father, The Prince of Peace." (Isaiah 9:6 KJV)

The prophecy of Isaiah about the child was 600 years before the birth of the Lord Jesus Christ. But we know that it was prophesied not to prove that the Bible is true or the absolute truth, because even before Isaiah's prophecy; God mentioned about Him in Genesis 3:15 already. The fulfillment of the prophecy about the birth of the Lord Jesus Christ is the reason why we celebrate Christmas. Compare Isaiah 7:14 and Matthew 1:21. In verses fourteen and twenty one, The Bible says; "14-Therefore the Lord himself shall give you a sign; Behold, a virgin shall conceive, and bear a son, and shall call his name Immanuel." "21- And she shall bring forth a son, and thou shalt call his name JESUS: for he shall save his people from their sins."

No wonder Christmas is being practiced almost all over the world. Some people are anxious of celebrating Christmas because of so many reasons; but for those who know the true meaning of Christmas, it's a joy and something very special. The true Biblical account of Christmas, and the true essence of Christmas is different from the world's mind set. Christmas is more commercialized and centered on animals, Santa Claus, old Saint Nick, the gifts and the three kings. Most Filipinos in the Philippines and many parts of the world celebrate Christmas with foods, drinks, caroling, and Christmas bonuses. In the Philippines, they are decorating their beautiful Christmas trees or lantern as early as September already. There's nothing wrong with us practicing the culture, the traditions, and other practices during Christmas days; but don't forget the true spirit of the celebration by focusing on the Celebrant- the Lord Jesus Christ. What is the true message of Christmas for you? How would you express that love and forgiveness that God had showed us in the Scriptures on that first Christmas day? Jesus is the light of the world, and He gave us the true message of Christmas by sharing us the love of the Father.

The light I bear on Christmas day,
A candle I share for the world to see;
I'm not alone His stars to shine
For the world to know that Jesus is mine.

"For God so loved the world, that he gave his only begotten Son, that whosoever believeth in him should not perish, but have everlasting life." (John 3:16 KJV)

Christmas *is the Love of God*

"And we have seen and do testify that the Father sent the Son to be the Saviour of the world." (I John 4:14 KJV)

Ely R. S.

I remember a beautiful song about Christmas from a play by "Psalty's Christmas Calamity". I love this part of the song; "Christmas is the time, Christmas is the time, Christmas is the time to love…" It's not just during Christmas, but everyday of our lives should be a time to love. Few years ago I wrote a song about love. My friend Macky Cordeniel helped me with the music and arrangement. "Love is the Reason" was recorded by my daughter to be used as a theme song for my radio program based in the Philippines and it can be heard on the internet. I love the message of the song, it minister's to my heart.

"Love is the reason, love is the key.
Love is what I long for; His love is all I need…
I know that love is everything; I know
that love is from God
I know that love bridges my soul to heaven,
God's love nailed Him on the tree…
Sin is the reason, sin brings misery,
His death is the answer, His love reaches me…
We are the reason… that put Him on a tree
But Christ is the answer His greatest love in me"

We cannot comprehend such love until we put out trust in Him and look up to the cross for our salvation. The Bible says: "Look unto me and be saved…"

The only reason for the season
Is for Christ to bring us salvation,
And honor the Father in what He has done;
It is to finish the work in due time;
The Holy Trinity planned for mankind,
He took upon Himself man's redemption.

"For when we were yet without strength, in due time
Christ died for the ungodly. 8- But God commendeth
his love toward us, in that, while we were yet sinners,
Christ died for us." (Romans 5:6; 8 KJV)

The Love of God the Father is the True Christmas Tree

The old hymn, "The Love of God" by Frederick M. Lehman
is a great picture of God's love although it's not even close
to the sacrifices Jesus did on the cross. The cross is the true
picture of the true Christmas tree for all the years, in all
generations, race and cultures.

What a beautiful song. No one can measure indeed or
describe it in words, tongues, or in any physical expression
of love. Our mind is limited in its capacity to comprehend
such *love*. It's really beyond our human comprehension.
Faith in the Lord and what He has done on the cross two
thousand years ago is the key to fully understand *His great
love for humanity.* And only as we *let* the Holy Spirit of God
convicts us of our sins, our hopelessness, and helplessness.
Not only God showed us His love through His Son, God
the Father was the one who executed such love on the cross.
No wonder when Jesus prayed in the garden of Gethsemane,
He asked the Father; "take this cup from me; yet not my
will, but yours be done." (Luke 22:42; I John 4:7- 12) The
Lord Jesus Christ by His death on the cross gave us the
Father's love, and such love should serve us an example for
us to follow. Notice the example of God and His love for
us. The Bible said: "For the wages of sin is death; but the

gift of God is eternal life through Jesus Christ our Lord."
(Romans 6:23 KJV)

The love of God was Christ's manifestation,
He shared at the cross of Calvary;
The angels cannot contend the emotions,
Jesus Christ died on the cross to end Satan's slavery...
The love so strong, the hell was shaken,
Because of His love we were forgiven;
The rich and poor or the miserable
Find hope in God through faith they've taken.

What is Your Acronym
for C-h-r-i-s-t-m-a-s?

"Therefore the Lord himself shall give you a sign;
Behold, a virgin shall conceive, and bear a son, and
shall call his name Immanuel." (Isaiah 7:14 KJV)

If you're a Christian and you don't believe in Christmas, or
you don't celebrate Christmas for some personal, cultural,
spiritual and other reasons; I believe you're missing a lot
of good things about Christmas and all the blessings of
Christmas. I've seen thousands of people came to know the
Lord because of Christmas messages or presentations. Why
not celebrate Christmas for the sake of the lost souls out
there who need Christ and salvation. There's nothing to lose
but something, and some precious souls to gain for Christ.

What is your acronym for C-H-R-I-S-T-M-A-S? I strongly
suggest you make your personal acronym about "C-H-R-
I-S-T-M-A-S" and make it be your guide, reminder, vow,
or just for fun in keeping the spirit of Christmas in your
heart or at home within the year. Check out the messages
and comments that I got from posting my wife's picture

on Facebook as she was putting up a Christmas tree and decorating in as early as July. The pictures may have been posted on first week of July and it was extremely hot. We hide their identity for privacy reasons and these are unedited. Some made a comment in their own language or dialect and we made an English translation for your convenience. Some of the comments were inappropriate and very personal and did not fit for the purpose and the celebration.

I. B B. said: "For what!!!!???month of july christmas???its weird!!!"

L .B. commented:- "Christmas in July,,, how awesome! Christmas is everyday."

M .B. said: "correct."

M .C. P (translated): "aga ng decoration nyo mate ah?enjoy agad yan." "You're decorating so early mate, eh? Enjoy right away..."

Z.B.: "aga naman ptr... tumatanggap na rin ako na regalo." "Hehehe. It's too early pastor... I'm accepting gifts already..."

J.B.: "Christmas in July?"

O.B.: "Don't get upset but putting up a christmas tree is a pagan practice and not bibilical...One of Satan's lie to decieive people. . . ..There's not such thing in the Bible."

@ O.B.:" I respect your stand, I believe it's fair enough for you to respect my stand. The words 'CHRISTmas tree' is not in the Bible, but I have seen people came to know the Lord by me using the CHRISTmas tree as an illustration and... a message to connect with people who needs the Lord. We used and practiced millions of things that are not in the Bible since birth. Don't replace Christ for CHRISTmas tree

and use CHRISTmas tree to draw people to Christ. We will
not let the devil use it to we're open minded."
A.B.B: "every day can be Christmas for Christians!"

My Acronym for Christmas:

C - Christ was born to die for you and for me. (John 1:11;
3:16; Romans 5:8) He came to die that we might live. "I
am crucified with Christ: nevertheless I live; yet not I, but
Christ liveth in me: and the life which I now live in the flesh
I live by the faith of the Son of God, who loved me, and gave
himself for me." (Galatians 2:20 KJV)

H - Hope, joy, and peace He brings for you today. (Luke
2:10- 14) The same hope, joy, and peace the Lord Jesus
Christ offered to the thief on the cross and to the rich young
ruler. (Mark 10:17- 31; Luke 23:39- 43) The rich man who
ridiculed Lazarus when they were both here on earth needs
the same hope, peace, and joy that Christians treasured in
their hearts. (Luke 16:19- 31) Jesus said; "Peace I leave with
you, my peace I give unto you: not as the world giveth, give
I unto you. Let not your heart be troubled, neither let it be
afraid." (John 14:27 KJV)

R - Rejoice ye Christians and all the world for God's
salvation is here. "How shall we escape, if we neglect so
great salvation; which at the first began to be spoken by the
Lord, and was confirmed unto us by them that heard him;"
(Hebrews 2:3; Matthew 1:21) When Jesus was born here
on earth for our sins; to some it was just another birth, to
others He was just a baby, and to the government officials,

He was an addition to a yearly census. To God, the angels, to Mary and Joseph, and to the whole world who believed in the God of the universe- the Lord's birth was something to rejoice upon and celebrate with honor and glory! When Joseph received the message from the angel of God; it was not just a message to calm down his fear, but also a reminder for him to *rejoice* and be *glad* because Jesus' birth will bring forgiveness and salvation for all men.

I - Invite your friends with haste unto God's place. You may invite them in your home and build a relationship with them in the spirit of Christmas. "Now when Jesus was born in Bethlehem of Judaea in the days of Herod the king, behold, there came wise men from the east to Jerusalem, 2- Saying, Where is he that is born King of the Jews? for we have seen his star in the east, and are come to worship him." (Matthew 2:1- 2 KJV)

S - Shepherds sang as they followed the stars in obedience to God's Word as the prophecy unfolded. You may not be a shepherd who followed the literal bright star of God on Christmas day; but you can follow Jesus- the Bright and Morning Star. Jesus is the light of the darkened world of sin. (John 1:1- 14)

T - Treasures were brought down by the wise men with a worshipful heart and spirit. We must do the same. Let's offer our hearts and our whole being to the King of kings! They offered Him honor, glory and praise. (Matthew 2:1- 11) The wise men (not the three kings) presented their gifts; they offered Him gold to our King of kings, and frankincense for the holy High Priest. He is the Priest of priests. The priest honored God with the smoke of incense. Myrrh- Jesus was a man of sorrow and grief. Jesus had to die for men as a sweet smelling sacrifice for God. Myrrh was used in embalming dead bodies.

M - Men of honor and wise in heart. They came in obedience and love for Christ. Do you honor God this Christmas or even on ordinary days? The wise men traveled with God's provision and protection. They have the Lord's bright star which serves as the G.P.S. (God's Path to the Savior) on their way to Bethlehem in a manger.

A - Angels' announcement about the birth of God's Son stirred the hearts of Christians, but fear on King Herod and his men. Fear is of the devil, and the enemy knew that he could destroy Joseph, Mary, King Herod, and the whole world by putting fear in their hearts. He will do the same to everyone. "For God hath not given us the spirit of fear; but of power, and of love, and of a sound mind." (II Timothy 1:7 KJV)

S - Savior, King of kings and Lord of lords. He was born in a humble place called Bethlehem, He died a cruel death at the cross of Calvary, and He is coming to reign. (Philippians 2:5-10) I wrote a short chorus about Christmas: "C"- for the Lord's Christmas tree, and with "H" -for *hope* to set men free. "R"- is for *resurrection* day. "I"- is for the *inspiration* of His word; "S" for the *Savior's* love for me. And "T" which stand for *truth* in God! Man needs Jesus because "*m*"- for

49

mankind, "*a*" is *all* and "*s*" for *sinners*! He came down for sinners and to set the captives free!

I don't know that much about Christmas tree,
And decorations of stars for all to see;
The shepherds in Bethlehem, they came to worship Him,
Our Christ, our Lord, the King of kings.
"When they saw the star, they rejoiced with
exceeding great joy." (Matthew 2:10 KJV)

JESUS- The Good Shepherd in the Manger

"I am the good shepherd: the good shepherd
giveth his life for the sheep." (John 10:11 KJV)

We picture the manger with a little baby on it, and with
Mary and Joseph watching over him. You have the animals,
the wise men, and the shepherds. The adorable baby on that
manger was Jesus the good Shepherd. Who is Jesus to you
personally? The acronym S-H-E-P-H-E-R-D may help us
understand and know more about our good Shepherd- the
Lord Jesus Christ.

S - Savior of the world. Jesus is the savior of the world and
He is coming again. (Titus 2:13- 14) Isaiah wrote: "For I am
the LORD thy God, the Holy One of Israel, thy Saviour..."
(Isaiah 43:3; 11 KJV)

H - Healer of all kinds of diseases: be it physical, spiritual,
emotional, mental, or psychological. "I will put none of
these diseases upon thee… for I am the LORD that healeth
thee." (Exodus 15:26; Psalm 100:3 KJV)

E - Eternal God. Jesus is from everlasting to everlasting. "The eternal God is thy refuge, and underneath are the everlasting arms..." (Deuteronomy 33:27 KJV)

P - Peace. Jesus is the Prince of peace. "The everlasting Father, The Prince of Peace..." (Isaiah 9:6- 7 KJV)

H - Hope. Jesus is our only hope and our blessed hope. "Looking for that blessed hope, and the glorious appearing of the great God and our Saviour Jesus Christ." (Titus 2:13 KJV)

E - Elohim. Jesus is the second person of the Holy Trinity. (Genesis 1:1) Scofield Bible made an excellent commentary and study about the Trinity especially on Genesis chapter one.

R - Redeemer. Praise God our Redeemer is alive and He reigns as King of kings and Lord of lords. "For I know that my redeemer liveth" or "Let the words of my mouth, and the meditation of my heart, be acceptable in thy sight, O LORD, my strength, and my redeemer." (Job 19:25; Psalm 19:14; Isaiah 54:5 KJV)

D - Deliverer. "The LORD is my rock, and my fortress, and my deliverer." (Psalm 18:2 KJV) The angels proclaimed Jesus' birth to the shepherds on that cold and glorious night. Jesus was visited by the shepherds on His birth. "And there were in the same country shepherds abiding in the field, keeping watch over their flock by night. 9- And, lo, the angel of the Lord came upon them, and the glory of the Lord shone round about them: and they were sore afraid. 10- And the angel said unto them, Fear not: for, behold, I bring you good tidings of great joy, which shall be to all people. 11- For unto you is born this day in the city of David a Saviour, which is Christ the Lord. 12- And this shall be a sign unto you; Ye shall find the babe wrapped in swaddling clothes, lying in a manger. 13- And suddenly there was with the angel a multitude of the heavenly host praising God, and saying, 14- Glory to God in the highest, and on earth peace, good will toward men." (Luke 2:8- 14 KJV)

The shepherds left their flock to come and worship the Shepherd of the shepherds. The shepherds sacrificed their time, their job, and only treasure (the flock) for Jesus' sake. They believed on the Shepherd in the manger who knows His sheep and understand their proneness to wander away and get lost. (John 10:3, 14) He knows our thirst and our infirmities. We know Him as our Shepherd, we hear His voice and we follow Him. The shepherds were Jesus' disciples because they heard His voice and followed His star to worship Him. (John 10:3- 4; 27) The shepherds walked for miles to see the baby Jesus in a manger. The Shepherd of shepherds came down from heaven to give His life for our sins on the cross of Calvary. (John 10:9- 15)

"A Psalm of David. The LORD is my shepherd; I shall not want. 2- He maketh me to lie down in green pastures: he leadeth me beside the still waters." (Psalm 23:1- 2 KJV)

Jesus is the Shepherd from a manger
God sent Him to die for sinner;
He sacrificed to please the Father
For Him alone and there's no other

The Passover- His birthday!

"Then Jesus six days before the passover came to Bethany,
where Lazarus was which had been dead, whom he
raised from the dead." (John 12:1; 20- 21 KJV)

I heard a story about a boy who was celebrating at a huge
birthday party. Everyone was busy, excited and having a
good time. They had food, drinks, and candies on the
table. The unwrapped gifts were set on beautiful settings
by the hallway. They had good and loud music, and great
festivity. While everybody was having fun and enjoying
their time together, the dad went to the microphone and
asked: "Where is John my son, the birthday celebrant?"
And there was an instant silence... It was a total misery
because they were celebrating the birthday party without
the birthday celebrant. It's a good picture of what happened
during the Passover. While the Jews were celebrating the
feast, they forgot about the Celebrant and the reason for
the celebration. It's a picture of our present Christmas
celebration. I wonder what could be in the Lord's heart and
mind as He looks down from heaven every Christmas day.
We have all this great celebration all over the world, but we
missed the point.

"We want to see Jesus," and they did. In this great feast, the
celebrant was there but unknown to the crowd. Jesus came

to the Passover for the celebration of what God has done during the time of Moses in the Old Testament. It was a picture of the Lord's salvation and the lamb is a picture of the Lord Jesus Christ. It's so unfortunate to know that they celebrate the feast of the Passover, but they ignore the Lamb. The Passover was supposed to center on the Lamb, but they could not even find Jesus and others don't know Him. The Greeks went to the Jewish celebration only to end their search for Him- Jesus the Lamb of the Passover. Jesus is the reason for the season. Christmas without Christ is empty. Who do you worship: the celebration or the celebrant? The heavenly hosts, the shepherds, the wise men, Mary and Joseph know Him, and they worshipped Him on that first Christmas day. How about you? Is *Jesus lost in the crowd on His own birthday?* Or we are just lost and we don't know what we're doing? How many Christmas have come and gone and we ignored Him in our big celebration of His birthday.

On His birthday, God watches us
eat, drink, play and pray,
But we forget the celebration of His day;
For us to know Him in a personal way;
God's gift for men is Christ who died to set men free.

"And there were certain Greeks among them
that came up to worship at the feast:

21- The same came therefore to Philip, which was
of Bethsaida of Galilee, and desired him, saying,
Sir, we would see Jesus." (John 12:20- 21 KJV)

The Comparison on Jesus with King Solomon

"The fear of the LORD is to hate evil: pride, and arrogance, and the evil way, and the forward mouth, do I hate. 14- Counsel is mine, and sound wisdom: I am understanding; I have strength. 15- By me kings reign, and princes decree justice. 16- By me princes rule, and nobles, even all the judges of the earth." (Proverbs 8:13- 16 KJV)

The book of Proverbs was penned by *King Solomon.* His name means *peaceable* which shows in his character, both of his spirit and of his life, and how he ruled his kingdom. He was different from his father David. David's life was full of troubles, while Solomon lived quietly and peaceably with his fellow men. We must maintain a peaceful and quiet life. Solomon was identified with King David, which means that he was in the lineage of the promised Messiah. He was the son of David. Jesus Christ was called "the Son of David" "The Son of Man" "The Son of God" and "The Only Begotten Son" in the New Testament. King Solomon was blessed with so much wealth, wisdom, and worldly accomplishments, but was a womanizer and addicted to wine. Our present generation calls it alcoholism, but the Bible calls it drunkenness. Jesus is holy, perfect, and sinless, and He has no weakness, but He came for the weak and hopeless.

Solomon lived in sin, but Jesus Christ died for our sins. Solomon was a son of a prayerful father and was born in a kingdom. Jesus Christ was from the kingdom of heaven, He prayed for us to the Father to draw us to Him. Solomon accumulated so much wealth, but Jesus Christ left the kingdom of heaven and became poor for us. "For ye know the grace of our Lord Jesus Christ, that, though he was rich, yet for your sakes he became poor, that ye through his poverty might be rich." (II Corinthians 8:9 KJV)

Jesus intercedes for us in our prayers. He is our only mediator and bridge to the Father. Apostle Paul wrote; "For this is good and acceptable in the sight of God our Saviour; 4- Who will have all men to be saved, and to come unto the knowledge of the truth. 5- For there is one God, and one mediator between God and men, the man Christ Jesus; 6- Who gave himself a ransom for all, to be testified in due time." (I Timothy 2:3- 6 KJV)

King Solomon was born in the majestic and fancy kingdom but Jesus was born in a manger. King Solomon stayed in his kingdom until his death, but Jesus Christ left His kingdom for death. Solomon was adorned and loved by his people and the kingdom. Jesus is worshipped, loved and adorned by the whole world from generation to generations. King Solomon was an heir of his father- King David. Jesus Christ reigns with God the Father and He gave power to the presidents, kingdoms, and kings, including King Herod who wanted to kill Him when He was a baby. Jesus Christ is our joint heir with the Father. (Roman 8:14- 18) Christ was called *the Son of David* and Solomon was a type of Christ. Solomon was the *king of Israel.* The Lord Jesus Christ is the King of kings and Lord of lords. Solomon was a good teacher and it shows in the book of Proverbs; he said on many occasions, "Hear my instructions…" or "Listen to my instruction…" Jesus is the Teacher of teachers. King Solomon was a man of wisdom and knowledge, but Jesus is the source of all wisdom and knowledge, including Solomon's wisdom and knowledge. It was God who gave it all to him. And Solomon's wisdom excelled the wisdom of all the children of the east country, and all the wisdom of Egypt. 31- For he was wiser than all men; than Ethan the Ezrahite, and Heman, and Chalcol, and Darda, the sons of Mahol: and his fame was in all nations round about." (I Kings 4:30- 31; 10:24 KJV) Solomon fed the children of Israel, but Jesus feed the whole world from generation after generations. "Solomon shared his knowledge about medicine, human principles, and philosophy in life, but Jesus is the healer and the only source of every good gifts.

Solomon was known and great among his people, but Jesus is the greatest to all people of every color, of every race, in every tongue and nation, and to every generation. Solomon can be compared to a man from age to age, but we cannot compare Jesus for He is God- the second person of the Holy Trinity. King Solomon talked about Him and he looked forward of meeting Jesus in heaven. Jesus Christ came down to die for Solomon's sins and our sins. This Christmas, let us remember Jesus who was born in Bethlehem, but He died at the cross of Calvary because of His love for you and for me. Solomon wrote; "I love them that love me; and those that seek me early shall find me" (Proverbs 8:17 KJV)

To compare my Lord to a human being,
Don't take it as an insult to Him as King of kings;
Christ is amazing in His love, in His
life and in His suffering,
And may your Christmas be full of God's love.

He Called His Name- "JESUS"

"And knew her not till she had brought forth her firstborn
son: and he called his name JESUS." (Matthew 1:25 KJV)

It was not Joseph who had the idea about the name. It was
the angels who gave him (Joseph) the name, but the origin
was from the heart of God. Christmas was God's idea, and
naming the child was God the Father's idea as well. When
I was growing up, I was so frustrated with my name. I
don't actually like my name because I thought I was the
only "Ely" in the world and the world to come. I thought
"Eli" in the Old Testament was the first and I would be
the last "Eli" ever. But here in Michigan, I have a friend
who loves the Lord and his name is "Eli". If I would be
given the opportunity to ask Joseph about the name; my
question would be: "When you gave Jesus that name, what
was your feeling?" Joseph called His name Jesus, because
He is the Savior of the world. He is our mediator and high
priest. The writer of the book of Hebrews said; "Now of the
things which we have spoken this is the sum: We have such
an high priest, who is set on the right hand of the throne of
the Majesty in the heavens." (Hebrews 8:1 KJV)

We must *accept* Jesus as our savior and trust Him as the *only*
high priest who can stand and mediate for us in the holy of

holies, in the kingdom of our Father. Jesus is our advocate to the Father. "Joseph called His name Jesus, because He is the author and finisher of our faith". Jesus is the name that will save us from our sins and the eternal damnation in hell. (Hebrews 12:1- 3; Philippians 2:9- 10; I John 2:1- 2) I get upset every time I hear people use the name of the Lord in vain. I get upset and grieved when I hear people use the name "Jesus" in substitute for cursing and swearing. The first time the word "Jesus" was mentioned in the Bible specifically in the New Testament was when the angel of the Lord gave Joseph and Mary the name for the child. The same way God did to Elisabeth when the angel of the Lord appeared to Zacharias, and informed him about his wife having a baby and they called his name "John". The name "Jesus" and "John" are blessed names, because it all came from the heart and mouth of God. Before their names touched the surface of the earth and were used by sinful men, it was made in heaven and was specially delivered by an angel from the throne of God to the mouth of sinful men. "And she shall bring forth a son, and thou shalt call his name JESUS: for he shall save his people from their sins." (Matthew 1:21 KJV)

> I know a name that's full of love,
> A name identified with sacrifice;
> In the name of Jesus will I be satisfied,
> Because He is the one who sanctified.

> "Looking unto Jesus the author and finisher of
> our faith; who for the joy that was set before him
> endured the cross, despising the shame, and is set

down at the right hand of the throne of God." "And
Joseph Call His Name Jesus, because He came
to set us free and to forgive us of our sins."

"21- And she shall bring forth a son, and thou
shalt call his name JESUS: for he shall save his
people from their sins." 36- "If the Son therefore
shall make you free, ye shall be free indeed."
(Hebrews 12:2, Matthew 1:21; John 8:36 KJV)

Jesus Was Born in Bethlehem… But He Was Too Big and Mighty for Bethlehem

"He was too big and mighty for Bethlehem…" those are the
words of Dr. J. Vernon McGee. Not only that Jesus was too
big for Jerusalem, but for the whole world to contain Him.
He is God, and He came down in the flesh. He humbled
Himself and became obedient to God's will so we can learn
to be obedient to His will. Most of all, the world of sin could
be saved and be forgiven. (Philippians 2:5- 10)

In his booklet *When God Became Man*, Dr. J. Vernon
McGee wrote: "The Greek language allows us to put it more
specifically and, I think, more accurately. 'The Word was
born flesh.' Turn this over in your mind for a moment. Here
comes God out of eternity, already the Ancient of Days; but
He also came to Bethlehem, a little baby thing that made
a woman cry. And notice that John's Gospel does not even
mention His birth in Bethlehem. Do you know why? He
is talking about One who is too big for Bethlehem. Out of
eternity, the Word became flesh." "But thou, Bethlehem

Ephratah, though thou be little among the thousands of Judah, yet out of thee shall he come forth unto me that is to be ruler in Israel; whose goings forth have been from of old, from everlasting."(Micah 5:2) Before Jesus was born, the Lord himself *prophesied* of the coming Messiah already. (Genesis 3:15) The Lord also *prepared* the coming of the Lord Jesus Christ. (John 1:18- 33) He also designated and marked the *place* where He, the Messiah, would be born. (Micah 5:2) The Father commanded the angels to inform and appoint the *persons* who would be involved in the birth of Christ. (Matthew 1:16-25) The Holy Trinity had it *planned* even before the foundation of the world. (John 1:1-18) And the Holy Trinity had a *purpose* as recorded in Matthew 1:21: "for he shall save his people from their sins."

What would people think of you if you're from a little town of Bethlehem and grew up in Nazareth? There are times when I'm out of state or out of the country, and when people ask me where I'm from, I say; "I'm from Detroit, Michigan." Some will show a negative facial expressions or reactions, others share some negative remarks. I would sometimes make some follow-ups and say: "I'm from Taylor, Michigan; it's about twenty five to thirty minutes from Detroit." You can sense the switched on their facial reactions. Detroit is a beautiful place; it's like some big cities, they have their own issues. That's how people might have thought of Jesus before He was born, while He was growing up, and during His more than three years of ministry here on earth. (John 1:37- 50)

Jesus is the Savior of the world. He created the whole universe. He is the King of kings and the Lord of lords; but He was born in a manger with just a swaddling clothes wrapped over Him. He was born in a place so special in the heart of God. Matthew Henry said; "Beth-lehem signifies the house of bread, the fittest place for him to be born in who is the bread of life." Jesus is your House of Bread, would you trust Him today?

It doesn't matter if you're rich or poor;
God sees your heart and not your house;
Your poverty or prosperity;
In God's sight it's just like a day that passes away;
The place you live and the blessings you have,
God owns them all and you're nothing to Him;
When you stand before Him on judgment day…
What you have accomplished and what you
have today will only be washed away.

"And Joseph also went up from Galilee, out of the city of Nazareth, into Judaea, unto the city of David, which is called Bethlehem; because he was of the house and lineage of David." (Luke 2:4 KJV)

Christmas- From the Old Testament Prophecies to Jesus on the Cross

"And I will put enmity between thee and the woman, and between thy seed and her seed; it shall bruise thy head, and thou shalt bruise his heel." (Genesis 3:15 KJV)

Adam, Eve, and Satan did not have any idea of what they heard in the Garden of Eden when God the Father first prophesied about the coming Messiah. They did not even know that God was talking about His death, which would be impossible to happen unless Christ would be born in the flesh. (Philippians 2:5- 10) In our own times and terms- God was talking about Christmas and Holy week. In his book *God's Plan Through the Ages*, C. A. Chader wrote: "What was the purpose of the incarnation of Christ?" He came:

1) - To bruise Satan and to break his power. (Genesis 3:15; John 12:31; I John 3:8)
2) - To reveal and declare God. (John 1:18; 14:8-10; Colossians 1:15; 2:9; Heb. 1:2- 3)
3) - To fulfill and complete the law and the prophets. (Matt. 5:17- 18; Luke 24:44- 47; John 19:28- 30; Romans 10:4; Ephesians 2:14-15)
4) - To redeem Israel from the curse of the law. (Galatians 3:13; 4:4-5)
5) - To become a substitutionary sacrifice for the sin of mankind. (Isaiah 53:5-7; 10; 12; Mark 10:45; II Corinthians 5:19- 20)
6) - To save individual sinners. (Matthew 1:21; Luke 19:10; I Timothy 1:15)
7) - To destroy death and the domain of death. (I Corinthians 15:24- 26; Revelations 1:17- 18) Observe that the first and the last of the purposes of the incarnation are still awaiting completion in connection with the Second Coming of Christ and the things that will follow thereafter. All the other

purposes have either been completely fulfilled, or are being fulfilled little by little in the same measure as by the Spirit Jesus is being revealed to men, and sinners are saved by the blood of His cross. Next we ask: How was this sevenfold purpose fulfilled in connection with the First Advent of Christ? We answer:

1) - Through the divine, supernatural virgin birth of Jesus.
2) - Through His holy, flawless, sinless life.
3) - Through His atoning, substitutionary death on the cross.
4) - Through His glorious, victorious resurrection, which carried with it His ascension and enthronement at the right hand of the Majesty on high. On this four-fold, four-square rock foundation rests our salvation, which is confirmed by the unchangeable Word of God, as well as by the definite, joyous, living experience of countless multitudes, which cannot be gain, said or refuted."

The fulfillment of the prophecies is great, and the results and what it has done to humanity from generations after generations can't be described in *words*. We have the empty manger, the empty cross, and the empty tomb for the empty hearts! The fulfillment of the prophecies is not just about the fulfillment of it, it's about God's plan for the ages and God's plan for every human being that would be born in this world and the world to come- the future generations.

It reveals who God is and it reveals His truth and the truth of the Word of God.

The Genealogy of Jesus

A Sunday school kid made a comment regarding him getting bored reading all the names, the kings, and their kingdoms in the books of I and II Chronicles, and I and II Kings in the Old Testament. He said: "I don't care about their names, the kings and the kingdoms…" One Christmas day, a Sunday school teacher assigned Matthew chapter one as their reading assignment few weeks before Christmas. One of his Sunday school students came to him the next Sunday, irritated and disappointed because they gave them the reading assignment that didn't really make sense! The Sunday school teacher asked him why it didn't make sense to him, and what made him so irritated and disappointed? The student said: "Because all I've read were 'names', 'begat', and 'generations'. The word *'begat'* ends on Matthew chapter one verse sixteen. And it says; "And Jacob begat Joseph the husband of Mary, of whom was born Jesus, who is called Christ." The teacher said; "That was the point!" The student was surprised to hear what his teacher said to him! The student asked with curiosity at this time: "What do you mean of "that was the point, I don't understand and I don't get it?" The teacher replied, "That was the point where the genealogy had to end, and that was the point where Jesus would make a new beginning." Indeed, God the Father put an end to the genealogy which ushered to the birth of the Messiah. Jesus would start a new beginning and a generation of the "church" and "grace." Matthew chapter one verse sixteen may not make sense to many. For those who look forward to God's plan and the coming Messiah; the genealogy and its end is the key to the New Testament era, the key to Christ's birth, life, death, and the key to His resurrection and ascension. It is the door to the church age because Jesus is the one who will turn the key to Peter.

Jesus is the key to everything in the New Testament. It is not just important, but it is of necessity, of which the Holy Spirit of God made Matthew penned the genealogy of Jesus as the fulfillment of the prophecy of His birth and for our enlightenment. (Genesis 3:15; Galatians 4:4) The Holy Spirit of God revealed the names of the four women in the genealogy of the Lord Jesus Christ in the first chapter of the book of Matthew. It's interesting to know of our Lord not being ashamed of His roots or ancestry. It's a joy to know that Jesus was also from the lineage of Booz of Rachab and Ruth. The Bible says; "And Salmon begat Booz of Rachab; and Booz begat Obed of Ruth; and Obed begat Jesse." (Matthew 1:5 KJV) It means they were strangers to the commonwealth of Israel. The Bible says; "That in the ages to come he might show the exceeding riches of his grace in his kindness toward us through Christ Jesus." (Ephesians 2:7 KJV) Again Paul said; " That at that time ye were without Christ, being aliens from the commonwealth of Israel, and strangers from the covenants of promise, having no hope, and without God in the world: 13- But now in Christ Jesus ye who sometimes were far off are made nigh by the blood of Christ. 14- For he is our peace, who hath made both one, and hath broken down the middle wall of partition between us; 15- Having abolished in his flesh the enmity, even the law of commandments contained in ordinances; for to make in himself of twain one new man, so making peace; 16- And that he might reconcile both unto God in one body by the cross, having slain the enmity thereby." (Ephesians 2:12- 16 KJV) We can see and witness for ourselves the grace of God even in genealogy.

The Canaanites were Israel's and the Lord's enemy in the Old Testament times. Read Joshua chapter nine to chapter eleven verses one to five. First, Booz of Rachab was from Canaan which was Moses' and Joshua's enemy. The Lord commanded Joshua to conquer their land as it was promised to Moses before he died. The Bible says; "And they answered Joshua, and said, Because it was certainly told thy servants, how that the LORD thy God commanded his servant Moses to give you all the land, and to destroy all the inhabitants of the land from before you, therefore we were sore afraid of our lives because of you, and have done this thing." (Joshua 9:24 KJV) All the land and the inhabitants of Canaan were not spared from the Lord's commands to Moses and Joshua. God can use people from Canaan and a harlot? Wow! God is amazing! He doesn't look at your background, your ethnicity or race and the color of your skin. God can use anyone, at anytime, from anywhere. God used even His enemy and the undeserved for His glory and to accomplish His will and purpose. It should serve as an encouragement for us sinners, gentiles, and undeserved!

The Syrophoenician Woman Tried to Re-connect with Jesus through His Lineage

In Matthew chapter fifteen, we have here the story of the woman from Canaan who came to the Lord Jesus Christ for help. She was called the Syrophoenician woman by some Bible scholars like C. I. Scofield. According to Unger's Bible Dictionary by Merril F. Unger: "*Syrophoenician* (si-ro-fe-ni-shan), a general name (Mark 7:26) of female inhabitant of the northern portion of Phoenicia, popularly called Syrophoenicia, by reason of its proximity to Syria and its absorption by conquest into that kingdom. The woman of Syrophoenicia applied to Jesus to heal her afflicted daughter, who was possessed with a demon. When she came near to him and worshipped, saying, "Lord help me," he replied, "It is not meet to take the children's bread and cast it to dogs." Whether this was to try her faith, or to show that at that time his work and mission were among Israel, is hard to determine. Her faith, however, was great and met its merited reward in the cure of her daughter. Matthew 15:22 calls her a *"woman of Canaan"* being in respect to her nationality, in common with the Phoenicians, a descendant of Canaan."

I love to preach about *faith* with Matthew 15:21- 28 as my text. The Syrophoenician woman came to Jesus one day and she prayed to Jesus for mercy. The woman was consistent with her prayer when she cried out unto Jesus saying: "Have mercy on me, O Lord, thou son of David; my daughter is grievously vexed with a devil." (Matthew 15:22 KJV) The woman emphasized in her prayer the roots of the Lord Jesus Christ when she said, "O Lord, thou son of David." Does she want Jesus to look back to His lineage and at the same time make Him aware that she too came from the same ancestry or roots? We cannot read what's in her mind and especially the Lord's mind. I don't know what's on the Lord's mind when He answered her not a word. But I'm very much sure that Jesus has a purpose and it was for His honor and glory. The Lord's silence was even misinterpreted by the disciples. The Bible says, "But he answered her not a word. And his disciples came and besought him, saying, Send her away; for she crieth after us." (Matthew 15:23 KJV) When Jesus did not answer any word, she cried a bit harder to get the Lord's attention. Some Christians have the same attitude toward God. We cry out to God in our prayers and if we don't get an answer or get what we wanted; we cry louder and harder with an expectation and anticipation of God hearing us and answering our prayers. God doesn't work that way and Jesus has a different purpose than what she and the disciples have in mind.

The reason for Jesus' silence could be because of what He said in verse 24. Jesus replied to her and said: "I am not sent but unto the lost sheep of the house of Israel." Now the connection is on the process, and it's working for her actually. Jesus was not playing favorites because He is a *just* God. He was not trying to be a racist, because He loves all the people of the world on the same level. The woman's persistency made her come closer to the throne of grace, and made her worship Christ with humility and prayer when she said: "Lord, help me." Notice the Lord's answer to her: "But he answered and said, It is not meet to take the children's bread, and cast it to dogs." (Matthew 15:26 KJV)

Jesus was trying to take her back to her roots. It was the other way around. Jesus was actually the one who tried to take her back to her roots. Jesus tried to make her realized that she was not a Jewess, but a gentile, from Canaan- the enemy of Israel. She was from the Syrophoenician group of people. She was an enemy of the Jews. I like the answer of the woman when she said: "Truth, Lord: yet the dogs eat of the crumbs which fall from their masters' table." (Matthew 15:27 KJV)

We came and serve the same Master, and we eat the same food from the same hands. The only difference is how the food is distributed by our Master and King, handed upon or served and given. The same mercy has the same grace from the same Master and God. "Then Jesus answered and said unto her, O woman, great is thy faith: be it unto thee even as thou wilt. And her daughter was made whole from that very hour." (Matthew 15:28 KJV) The Lord answered her prayers and He honored her faith. The woman may have been thinking of her forefathers and the Lord's forefathers as being from the same roots when she approached the Lord Jesus Christ. Jesus did not look at her race and origin, but her faith in Him. Let's go back to the Old Testament believers. Here Matthew mentioned the lineage of Jesus. "And Salmon begat Booz of Rachab; and Booz begat Obed of Ruth; and Obed begat Jesse." (Matthew 1:5 KJV) Ruth and Esther are not strangers or unfamiliar names for many Christians and Jews. They played the role of preserving the lineage of Jesus by preserving Israel, the chosen nation of God the Father. They stood up for what is right and in the will of God. They risked their lives for the sake of

God's people- the Jews. God has a special plan way over from preserving His chosen nation, but He was also looking forward to providing a Lamb for the salvation of the Jews and gentiles by the death of His own dear Son. I believe God honored them because of their humility and faith in the Lord.

Ruth and Esther may have been thinking of the present generations during those times, but God was thinking of you and of the whole world when He preserved and protected His chosen people. If you will read the genealogy of Jesus over and over, you will begin to see the blessings, the grace, and mercy of God. You will also see the hands of God in His people, and how God has preserved the lineage of Jesus in spite of persecutions, atrocities, hates, and the desire of the enemy to eliminate the Jews. Even after His birth, King Herod wanted to kill Him. Notice what the Bible says; "And being warned of God in a dream that they should not return to Herod, they departed into their own country another way. 13- And when they were departed, behold, the angel of the Lord appeareth to Joseph in a dream, saying, Arise, and take the young child and his mother, and flee into Egypt, and be thou there until I bring thee word: for Herod will seek the young child to destroy him. 14- When he arose, he took the young child and his mother by night, and departed into Egypt: 15- And was there until the death of Herod: that it might be fulfilled which was spoken of the Lord by the prophet, saying, Out of Egypt have I called my son. 16- Then Herod, when he saw that he was mocked of the wise men, was exceeding wroth, and sent forth, and slew all the children that were in Bethlehem, and in all the coasts thereof, from two years old and under, according to the time which he had diligently inquired of the wise men."(Matthew 2:12- 16 KJV)

Some Bible scholars may call the books of I and II Chronicles and the books of I and II Kings "the chosen books of the theocracy". But they're more than just "the chosen books", but the books of the Lord and His chosen people. Those are special books for the Jews because of the history of the kings, and the kingdom of Israel and neighboring countries. The genealogy of the Lord Jesus Christ in the book of Matthew has a solid connection into it. God revealed His plan, His purpose, His people and the prophecy of the incarnation of the Lord Jesus Christ as recorded on the said books! King David and King Solomon are the pictures of the Lord Jesus Christ. It shows us about the history of the worst, and the best kings that reigned in Israel and the neighboring countries. It also talks about the kingdoms and its people. The genealogy defines the coming King, His roots and it makes us look forward to His coming and His coming Kingdom. Most importantly it also made us look back to His birth, His death, and His burial by faith.

The Prophets Wrote of Israel's Captivity and the Coming Messiah

As the Lord prospered the Israelites, the people became rebellious and self-sufficient. It's a good picture of this present generation. The Lord spread out the Jewish people from their beloved country because of their stubbornness. They lost tracked of their roots, of their family trees, and of their closest kin. The Babylonian captivity could be one of the stages in Israel's history which ushered them to the most humbling stages in their life, country, and people. (Nehemiah 1:1- 11; Ezra 1:1- 4) Daniel as a man of God and a man of wisdom may already have the idea of the plight of his people. It was the revelation of the Holy Spirit and the writings of Jeremiah the prophet. The Bible says, "Therefore thus saith the LORD of hosts; Because ye have not heard my words, 9- Behold, I will send and take all the families of the north, saith the LORD, and Nebuchadrezzar the king of Babylon, my servant, and will bring them against this land, and against the inhabitants thereof, and against all these nations round about, and will utterly destroy them, and make them an astonishment, and an hissing, and perpetual desolations. 10- Moreover I will take from them the voice of mirth, and the voice of gladness, the voice of the bridegroom, and the voice of the bride, the sound of the millstones, and the light of the candle. 11- And this whole land shall be a desolation, and an astonishment; and these nations shall serve the king of Babylon seventy years. 12- And it shall come to pass, when seventy years are accomplished, that I will punish the king of Babylon, and that nation, saith the LORD, for their iniquity, and the land of the Chaldeans, and will make it perpetual desolations."(Jeremiah 25:8- 12 KJV)

The prophet Daniel saw the plight of Israel and plan of the Lord Jesus Christ. Daniel wrote about the Messiah, His birth and His death. Daniel even outlined the timetable which no one in the books of the Old Testament ever pictured and put in words so great and enlightening. "23- At the beginning of thy supplications the commandment came forth, and I am come to show thee; for thou art greatly beloved: therefore understand the matter, and consider the vision. 24- Seventy weeks are determined upon thy people and upon thy holy city, to finish the transgression, and to make an end of sins, and to make reconciliation for iniquity, and to bring in everlasting righteousness, and to seal up the vision and prophecy, and to anoint the most Holy. 25- Know therefore and understand, that from the going forth of the commandment to restore and to build Jerusalem unto the Messiah the Prince shall be seven weeks, and threescore and two weeks: the street shall be built again, and the wall, even in troublous times. 26- And after threescore and two weeks shall Messiah be cut off, but not for himself: and the people of the prince that shall come shall destroy the city and the sanctuary; and the end thereof shall be with a flood, and unto the end of the war desolations are determined." (Daniel 9:23- 26)

Cyrus King of Persia played a special role in the returned of God's people from captivity. (II Chronicles 36:22- 23; Ezra 1:1- 4) The prophet Daniel wrote; "17- As for these four children, God gave them knowledge and skill in all learning and wisdom: and Daniel had understanding in all visions and dreams. 18- Now at the end of the days that the king had said he should bring them in, then the prince of the eunuchs brought them in before Nebuchadnezzar. 19- And the king communed with them; and among them all was found none like Daniel, Hananiah, Mishael, and Azariah: therefore stood they before the king. 20- And in all matters of wisdom and understanding, that the king inquired of them, he found them ten times better than all the magicians and astrologers that were in all his realm. 21- And Daniel continued even unto the first year of king Cyrus." (Daniel 1:17- 21)

Mister Matthew Henry wrote; "Industry is the way to preferment. How long the other three were about the court we are not told; but Daniel, for his part, continued to the first year of Cyrus (v. 21), though not always alike in favour and reputation. He lived and prophesied after the first year of Cyrus; but that is mentioned to intimate that he lived to see the deliverance of his people out of their captivity and their return to their own land. Note, sometimes God favours his servants that mourn with Zion in her sorrows to let them live to see better times with the church than they saw in the beginning of their days and to share with her in her joys." The Lord by His grace, mercy, and providence used Daniel and the three Hebrews during the stages of God's plan and works for the freedom of His chosen people. They were the wise, knowledgeable, and influential men of God." "Then Arioch brought in Daniel before the king in haste, and said thus unto him, I have found a man of the captives of Judah, that will make known unto the king the interpretation. 49- Then Daniel requested of the king, and he set Shadrach, Meshach, and Abednego, over the affairs of the province of Babylon: but Daniel sat in the gate of the king." (Daniel 2:25; 49) The Bible Collection

God in His due time which means in His own sovereign rule and timing sent forth His Son the Lord Jesus Christ. He was born of a virgin in due time. (Galatians 4:3- 5) In the Bible College where I finished my theology, we had a subject about the books of Daniel and Revelation. We were asked to do research about the 70th week of Daniel. It's about the prophecies regarding the restoration of the temple which would be about 483 years unto the crucifixion of the Lord Jesus Christ. It was fun and sometimes becomes a mind twister for me and complicated because of all the numbers, additions, and multiplications. Math is my weak point and I thought I could run away from numbers or math subjects because I'm in a Bible College. Obviously I did not get to run away from it, and it was my toughest subject in my whole seminary life. But Daniel through God's leading and by the moving of the Holy Spirit revealed the secrets of God about the due time of the coming Messiah, and the day of His death. The math issue was a struggle, but the results and fulfilment of the prophecies are great, it's enlightening and a blessing.

The Prophecy- Jesus will destroy Satan at the Cross of Calvary (Genesis 3:15)

His race and nation
(Genesis 12:1- 3; Micah 5:2)————(Romans 9:4- 10)

Jesus is from the tribe of Judah
(Genesis 49:8- 12)————(Luke 2:3- 4)

Jesus' seeds and family
(Isaiah 9:6- 10; 7:13- 17)————(Luke 2:3- 4)

The place of His birth
(Micah 5:2)————(Matthew 2:1- 8)

Satan has tried everything he can to destroy the lineage of Jesus. He tried to destroy Him by destroying His race, His nation, His family and His birth. Satan knows that He will be defeated in Calvary and he will be destroyed from there. The children of Israel need to come out of captivity and be identified as a nation- a nation of God. God made a promise to Abraham about His blessing upon them and making them a great nation. (Genesis 12:1- 3) God made a step by humbling them through captivity and leading them to God's purpose through the Lord Jesus Christ. (Galatians 4:4) The Jews during those times may not have the clear picture of what the Bible says about them and what God had for them in the future. It was like an unsolved puzzle for them. No wonder they were stiff-necked from the time of Moses until the Babylonian captivity. Even in such a time where persecutions and death was a part of their day to day life.

The devil tried everything, and every angle in life in any way he could to destroy the child and God's plan for the ages. He tried to destroy Israel's heritage from the time of Moses when Pharaoh tried to kill all the children from two years old and below. The devil did it over and over during the Old Testament times, during the silent years, and in the New Testament era during the birth of the Lord Jesus Christ. And the invasion of Titus the Great to Jerusalem was part of his plan. Satan tried it again during the time of the Nazi's under the rule of Adolf Hitler in Germany when he killed more than 6 million Jews. Egypt was a place of refuge for Mary and Joseph. When Abraham went to Egypt, it was for comfort, for convenience, and wealth. When Joseph and Mary went to Egypt, it was because they were fleeing from Herod's evil desire and selfish, deadly, and ambitious plan to kill Jesus. Satan knows that his time is very near.

Ezekiel Wrote of God's Hand in His Chosen People

Ezekiel looked ahead on the time where God's hand would put them together through the Son of David- the Lord Jesus Christ. The Israelites prospered and they multiplied in foreign lands. They may have started their new homes and families while they were in exile in Babylon. It was sad because the reason of their captivity was because of their rebellion to God. They were servants, not only to those who put them in captivity, but also they were captives of their own sins. They were proud and they made God jealous because of their idolatry. They worshipped themselves and other gods. (Daniel 3:1- 27) It's a good picture of our present generation in which we would rather lose our roots, good culture, tribes and even country as long as we get the wealth we deeply desired. Sometimes we put our families and religious beliefs and stand in exchange to our own gods, evil works and bad deeds. We see God's hand, His sovereign will and His intervention for His people, Israel. We can see God's favor and God's plan on His chosen people by opening the doors for them, and for their liberty or freedom. The good thing is we (the gentiles) became partakers of God's blessings, grace and mercy in lieu of them.

God used Cyrus, Nehemiah, Ezra, and even queen Esther to set them free, to preserve them and to bless them which absolutely leads to the genealogy of the Lord Jesus Christ. (Ezra 2:59) What would be your feeling as you watched on your widescreen television with thousands of children, babies and adults marching out of Babylon walking as a free nation after hundreds of years in captivity? If I did, I would just think of the mixed emotions of the people while marching out with songs of deliverance, and the marching bands playing "Glory, glory hallelujah; His truth is marching on..." I would not be surprised if tears flowed from their eyes and from the eyes of those who watched the Israelites' exodus. It would be like the Exodus of the children of Israel from Egypt. Some of them would leave their most beloved friends, job, memories, but God has a better plan for them and their roots. They will be identified with the God of Jacob and King David, as well as with the Lord Jesus Christ. We can be identified by our love for Christ. Our identification with Christ as His disciples is confirmed and expressed through water baptism. (II Corinthians 5:17;

John 3:1- 7; Romans 6:1- 23) The children of Israel were identified with God by their physical roots or by birth as the children of promised, but the Christians were identified with Christ by spiritual birth. It is our exodus from the world, from sin, from condemnation, from the hands of Satan to God, to heaven and to justification.

"JESUS is the Center of Christmas, Why Cancel It?"

"He came unto his own, and his own
received him not." (John 1:11 KJV)

The world celebrates Christmas with a different perspective. Some overlooked the *Christ* of Christmas. I was watching the movie *The Man Who Saved Christmas*. It's a true story of a man by the name of A.C. Gilbert. During World War II, the defense department asked Mr. Gilbert to open his toy factory for the United States government to use to manufacture war supplies. Thus, Mr. Gilbert let the government used his facilities, but during those times of hardship and war, the government wanted to cancel Christmas so people would start buying bonds instead of toys for Christmas. In one of their meetings Mr. A.C. Gilbert said, "If you cancel Christmas, you're cancelling hope." It's so sad to know that some Christians are cancelling Christmas because of some religious belief and practices, or because Christmas was identified with paganism.

An individual I knew a few years ago would not celebrate Christmas because he said, "The word Christmas is not in the Bible." Others don't celebrate Christmas for personal reasons. We respect other people's culture, traditions, and belief; but if you're a Christian, and you know that Christmas can draw people to the Lord; then I believe it's about time to ponder about it in your heart and consider the idea of celebrating it this time. Why cancel Christmas if Christmas could bring hope to the hopeless and love, joy, peace and forgiveness. I've seen hundreds of people came to know the Lord in Christmas functions, activities or concerts. It's better to celebrate and have fun. It's great to have one than not having Christmas at all. Jesus was born in the flesh and the modern generation calls it "Christ*mas*", and you better believe it! Jesus is the center of Christmas no matter how you celebrate it, and even if you don't believe on Christmas. Christmas is about Christ, His birth, and how God ushered Him to the cross of Calvary.

There was a woman who was from Michigan. She married a doctor from Iran who seemed to be so nice to her and her daughter. The family went to Iran for a vacation which leads to the husband's decision to live there for good. They made a movie about her life in Iran. In that movie "Not Without My Daughter", I was surprised to see the Iranian Muslims celebrating Christmas. It's so sad and ironic that some Baptist and Christians don't celebrate Christmas at all. It's unfortunate to know of individuals, churches, and Christian organizations playing the role of Scrooge of the modern society. We must stop those who play the role of Grinch and Scrooge. There are people and religious groups who try to destroy, distract, or discourage others from celebrating Christmas. These are the people who tried to quench the spirit and the joy of Christmas! Taking Christmas off from your lists of your holidays is like taking Christ out from your life, and from the best and most joyful celebration of the year.

If you believe that one day Christ was born...
There is no reason for you to ignore His birth;
Let us honor and praise Him for what He has done...
You have the reason to celebrate as what God has planned.

"And the Word was made flesh, and dwelt among us, (and we beheld his glory, the glory as of the only begotten of the Father,) full of grace and truth." (John 1:14 KJV)

The Prince of Peace in a Manger with a Mission from the Father

"For unto us a child is born, unto us a son is given: and the government shall be upon his shoulder: and his name shall be called Wonderful, Counsellor, The mighty God, The everlasting Father, The Prince of Peace." (Isaiah 9:6 KJV)

Evangelist Billy Graham in his book "Peace with God" wrote; "Peace can be experienced only when we have received divine pardon- when we have been reconciled to God and when we have harmony within, with our fellow man and especially with God." Men are willing to write a check in exchange for peace. "And the way of peace have they not known." (Romans 3:17) Jesus is our only source of peace. Six times in the New Testament He is called- "The God of Peace". Peace can only be experienced once we received the divine pardon from the Almighty and the Prince of peace. "Therefore being justified by faith, we have peace with God through our Lord Jesus Christ." (Romans 5:1) There have been wars in many countries including civil wars, wars between siblings and love ones, wars between husbands and wives, and wars at churches. The greatest war that is very active right now is between God and man. It's between God's holiness and man's wickedness. The other wars are the wars between God and Satan, and our warfare with the enemy as God's children. Notice what Paul said: "And the peace of God, which passeth all understanding, shall keep your hearts and minds through Christ Jesus." (Philippians 4:7 KJV)

When I was a teenager, I had a friend and a boss who was a millionaire. We used to go to restaurants and night clubs, and we would get drunk until the middle of the night or early morning. He was successful in his business but a failure in his family. His beautiful home, his successful and growing business, and our eating and drinking habits did not make us happy or give us peace of mind. At one time he even said to me: "I need peace and I want peace of mind, Ely." That's what the world needs. I recently was talking to a friend who is very successful in a restaurant business here in Michigan. He just came home from a vacation outside of the country. In our conversations regarding the success that he's enjoying with his business, he said, "I can't actually sleep at night and I have no peace of mind." He added; "There's so many things in my mind…"

You may have everything this world can offer,
But if your heart is empty and you struggle and suffer;
And you tried everything to satisfy your longing,
Jesus is the Prince of peace; He is the answer to your pain.

"Of the increase of his government and peace there shall
be no end, upon the throne of David, and upon his
kingdom, to order it, and to establish it with judgment
and with justice from henceforth even forever. The zeal of
the LORD of hosts will perform this." (Isaiah 9:14 KJV)

A troubled heart and minds are two of man's greatest
enemies. "Peace of mind", the 3 words with great impact
in people's lives. Millions of people are seeking it in money
and success. Millions of dollars are spent to attain peace.
The wealthy are willing to trade their wealth in exchange
for peace. The ungodly seek it in worldly wisdom, in wine,
in astrology, in works, in sex and gambling, or in temporal
things to gain peace, only to end their exploration for peace
in failure after failures.

In a complicated and confused world of greed and
selfishness, the prevailing principles are: "How can I have
more… and will it give me peace?" Millions of people are
looking for peace in the wrong place, wrong person, and
in a wrong perspective. Men are willing to write a check
in exchange for peace. Christians have found it. We have
found the secret of life. The source and the Prince of peace!
(Romans 3:17) Peace in the Bible is more than the absence of
war. "SHALOM" means "Peace: may you have no battles."
Jesus is the Only Source of Peace. We have peace with God.
(Romans 5:1) God is worthy of our peace. We must humbly

come to Him in repentance and be at peace with Him. (I Corinthians 14:33) We can also have the peace of God. Apostle Paul said: "And the peace of God, which passeth all understanding, shall keep your hearts and minds through Christ Jesus." (Philippians 4:7 KJV)

Christians have the peace of God in spite of problems, sicknesses, or losing a job. We have that peace which we can't, and will never understand until we see Him face to face. God is the God of peace, and our Savior is the Prince of peace. The Holy Spirit is the Spirit of peace. We need the peace of God because He is the God of peace. We need the Holy Spirit because He is the Spirit of peace. And we need the Lord Jesus Christ because He is the Prince of peace. (Galatians 5:22) If we are going to be a peacemaker, it is of necessity for us know God and draw upon this supply of peace from the throne of His grace.

Satan and sin is the worst enemy of peace. (Proverbs 16:7) We are the friend of God but we are the enemy of the world, the flesh, and the devil. I could not be at peace with God if there is sin in my life. We cannot be at peace with God and at the same time at peace with the world. As Christians, we're supposed to be "Ministers of Peace". The angels don't have any idea of what it means to have a troubled heart. Jesus knows our troubled spirit and our troubled heart and minds. (John 14:1- 6; 27) The angels announced "Peace on earth!" You can still experience the blessing of the peace of God when you're under stress or when you have so many burdens and cares. Again, Apostle Paul made it clear for us when he gave us these comforting words in Philippians 4:7. As followers of the Lord Jesus Christ, the peace of God is ruling in our hearts. (Colossians 3:15) We can serve our country and our Lord by being ministers of peace, by controlling our anger, by getting rid of our hatred and bitterness, and being at peace with our brethren. (Proverbs 18:19; Ephesians 4:25- 32)

Jesus set an example at the cross of Calvary when He humbled Himself and submitted to the will of the Father by His death on the cross. *Calvary is the Greatest Example of Making Peace with God...* At the cross of Calvary, we claim the promise of the Prince of peace for the whole world. It was the promise of forgiveness and freedom from our guilt! Those who abused and commercialized Christmas will someday stand before the Judge of judges. They will not stand before a baby in a manger, but before the Judge, King of kings and Lord of lords. It's not because of their attitude toward Christmas, but because they don't have the Prince of peace in their hearts. They will have no business in taking part to the true worship of the believers in heaven.

Those who take part in its celebration, but have no part in Him whose birthday is worthy of worship and praise deserved to be judged and be condemned! Jesus is the priceless Christ of Christmas! Satan is happy to see us celebrating His birthday, yet forget about His death and resurrection. People should have the same desire like the Greeks when they said, "Sir, we would see Jesus." The price of Christmas is Christ's death on the cross; without it, Christmas would just be a mere celebration of the people in the name of Christ. When we recognize Jesus' Kingship, we give him our worship. If you recognize Him as your Prince of peace, then give Him your praise.

Jesus Christ is Wonderful!

"And she brought forth her firstborn son, and wrapped him in swaddling clothes, and laid him in a manger; because there was no room for them in the inn." (Luke 2:7 KJV)

The Wonder of His Birth

His birth was first mentioned by the Lord Himself when God said: "And I will put enmity between thee and the woman, and between thy seed and her seed; it shall bruise thy head, and thou shalt bruise his heel." (Genesis 3:15 KJV) It was the first prophecy in the Bible from the mouth of God. It was the first promise of a Redeemer, a Savior. The Bible revealed the place of His birth. (Micah 5:2) His birth was prophesied by both major and minor prophets hundreds of years before He was born. (Isaiah 9:6; 7:13- 17) His birth was unique as compared to some of the greatest men and women who have lived since creation.

Imagine the day Jesus was born and think of the wise men, the shepherds, Mary and Joseph together with the animals. They were all in the spirit of worship. "And when they were come into the house, they saw the young child with Mary his mother, and fell down, and worshipped him: and when they had opened their treasures, they presented unto him gifts; gold, and frankincense, and myrrh." (Matthew 2:11

KJV) Jesus' birth was unique and different from the great men of the centuries because it is observed universally for more than 2,000 years. *Jesus' life was different from the great men of the centuries because:*

- He was completely man but He was sinless. (John 8:46)
- His works and ministry were unique.
- He healed the sick with his Words and raised Lazarus from the dead.
- He loves us in spite of our sinfulness. "He taketh away the sins of the world." (John 1:29)
- He cares for us and did miracles, and is still performing miracles in spite of our being unworthy.
- Jesus influenced the world from the time He was born until these present times and the time to come.
- He walked on the water and He walks with us every day: in the valley, to the mountains, and in the ocean of problems. He will be with us in our sufferings, until we meet Him face to face.

The Wonder in His Words (The Amazing Power of His Words)

- We were changed by His Words. (John 3:1- 7; II Corinthians 5:17)
- He spoke in parables. (Luke 18:1- 14)
- He rebuked people with love and compassion. (Mark 10:1- 32)
- He spoke with power. (Mark 4:36- 41)

- He caused the blind to see... It was the power of His Words of compassion. (Mark 10:46- 52)
- He raised the dead. (John 11:30- 45)
- He took control of nature with His Words. (Luke 21:33; Mark 4:36- 41)
- The devil trembles at His Word. (Matthew 4:1- 11; Mark 5:1-19) We sing His Words and we write songs, hymns, poems and spread His Words. We get encouraged and convicted of our sins by His Words.

The Wonder in His Death (He Died Not for Himself but for Us)

- He died not for Himself, but for us, for our sins. (Romans 5:8; 6:23 John 3:16; II Corinthians 5:21)
- He died for the salvation of mankind. (John 3:17)
- He died to give us hope. (Titus 2:10- 13)
- He died so we can live. (II Corinthians 5:21)
- He died, He was buried, and rose again the third day according to the Scriptures, and He's coming back. (I Corinthians 15:1- 7)
- He died for a purpose and with a purpose. (John 1:1- 14)
- He died with hope and in obedience to His Father's will, and for the sake of others. He died in humility and He died in due time. (John 19:30; Philippians 2:5- 11; Galatians 4:4)

The Wonder in His Kingship (He is a King but He Lived a Simple Life)

- He created the world, but He did not own a home when He was here on earth. "And Jesus said unto him, Foxes have holes, and birds of the air have nests; but the Son of man hath not where to lay his head." (Luke 9:58 KJV)

- He was rich but He became poor. (II Corinthians 8:9) He owns the cattle of the thousand hills, but He was buried in a borrowed tomb. "For every beast of the forest is mine, and the cattle upon a thousand hills." (Psalms 50:10) He is the King of kings and Lord of lords, but He was the Servant of men. Paul wrote; "Let this mind be in you, which was also in Christ Jesus: 6- Who, being in the form of God, thought it not robbery to be equal with God: 7- But made himself of no reputation, and took upon him the form of a servant, and was made in the likeness of men." (Philippians 2:5- 7 KJV)

- He came down and humbled Himself to love, but He was hated even of His own. (John 1:11) One thing is for sure, and this will never change: "His name is JESUS, for He will save His people from their sins." "And she shall bring forth a son, and thou shalt call his name JESUS: for he shall save his people from their sins. 22- Now all this was done, that it might be fulfilled which was spoken of the Lord by the prophet, saying, 23- Behold, a virgin shall be with child, and shall bring forth a son, and they shall call his name Emmanuel, which being interpreted is, God with us. 24- Then Joseph being raised from sleep did as the angel of the Lord had bidden him, and took unto him his wife: 25- And knew her not till she had brought forth her firstborn son: and he called his name JESUS." (Matthew 1:21- 25 KJV)

Jesus is Different from the Great Men of the Centuries (He Died and Rose Again the Third Day According to the Scriptures) (Acts 1:8- 11; 1I Corinthians 15:1- 10).

Jesus is Different from the Great Men of the Centuries (He Went Up to Heaven, He Promised that He is Coming Again) (I Thessalonians 4:14- 18; I Corinthians 15:50- 58)

He can be yours today if you will ask Jesus to come into your heart. He will make this Christmas a meaningful and memorable one.

The Greats in the Political Arena:

- Alexander the Great was a great leader and a great conqueror, but he died a miserable death. He left his power, wealth, and leadership without a promise of coming back to life and power.

- The then-president of the Philippines Ferdinand E. Marcos was a great leader. He was called the dictator by the Filipino people. He was smart and he accumulated a vast wealth in cash and gold. He died in Hawaii while in exile. He came home to the Philippines a frozen corpse. He lost his power, his position, and his possessions were sequestered by the Philippine government.

- The great leaders and presidents of countries such as Afghanistan, Iraq, Egypt, and others who were once powerful, wealthy, and some are corrupt leaders. And a killer like Adolf Hitler, they all died and lost their power, wealth, and influence. Some are remembered as the worst leaders of their country after their death.

The Great People with Financial Power:

These great people in their field with financial power either filed for bankruptcy or lost all their wealth for different reasons: According to an article found on Yahoo Voices, "Thomas Jefferson was one of the greatest and smartest of all Presidents of the United States. Unfortunately, he wasn't smart about money for his heirs. After his death, his estate Monticello and all his possessions, including 120 slaves, were auctioned off to help pay off $107,000 in debts (a fortune in 1826)".

The Angel's Ministries Before and After Christ's Birth!

"For unto you is born this day in the city of David a Saviour, which is Christ the Lord." (Luke 2:11 KJV)

The angel of God had a big part on first Christmas day. The heavenly hosts of God brought good tidings, announcements, and information regarding the Lord's birth. The angel's comfort and encouragement played a big role in the Lord's servants as they follow and obey God's will and God's Word. If the angel Gabriel is the closest angel in the throne of God, then there was no reason for them not to believe God's messenger.

- The angel proclaimed the birth of God's Son. "Then took he him up in his arms, and blessed God, and said, 29- Lord, now lettest thou thy servant depart in peace, according to thy word: 30- For mine eyes have seen thy salvation." (Luke 1:31; 2:11; 28- 30)
- The angel proclaimed the greatness of Jesus. "He shall be great, and shall be called the Son of the

Highest: and the Lord God shall give unto him the throne of his father David." (Luke 1:32 KJV)

- The angel proclaimed the authority of Jesus. "And he shall reign over the house of Jacob for ever; and of his kingdom there shall be no end." (Luke 1:33) "And to the angel of the church in Philadelphia write; These things saith he that is holy, he that is true, he that hath the key of David, he that openeth, and no man shutteth; and shutteth, and no man openeth." (Revelation 3:7 KJV)

- The angel announced that Jesus would be born of a virgin. (Luke 1:26- 32)

- The angel proclaimed that Jesus' birth will bring good tidings of great joy. "And the angel said unto them, Fear not: for, behold, I bring you good tidings of great joy, which shall be to all people." (Luke 2:10 KJV)

- The angel assured us that Jesus will bring peace on earth and goodwill toward men. "Glory to God in the highest, and on earth peace, good will toward men." (Luke 2:14 KJV)

- The angel proclaimed that Jesus is the King of an everlasting Kingdom. "And he shall reign over the house of Jacob for ever; and of his kingdom there shall be no end." (Luke 1:33 KJV)

- The angel assured and comforted Joseph, Mary, and the shepherds. It was the same message; "do not be afraid!" God has the same message for all of us 365 days a year: *"Fear not"*. (Matthew 1:20; Luke 1:30; 2:9- 10)

- The angel told Zacharias not to be afraid, and Zacharias was informed by the angel that Elisabeth his wife would bear a son and he shall call his name *"John."* He would prepare the way of the Lord. (Luke 1:13)
- The angel warned Joseph and Mary of the danger and the evil plot of King Herod. (Matthew 2:13- 15)

The Shepherds Were Appointed by the Angels

"And it came to pass, as the angels were gone away from them into heaven, the shepherds said one to another, Let us now go even unto Bethlehem, and see this thing which is come to pass, which the Lord hath made known unto us." (Luke 2:15 KJV)

There's no excuse for anyone who was called by God to a specific ministry. There's no excuse for believers when asked by the Lord to serve. Moses made some excuses and tried to get around God by his arguments, and personal inability, and weaknesses. (Exodus 3:1- 22; 3:1, 11- 17) Moses was more comfortable making excuses to God than following Him by faith and in His will. Imagine a church full of shepherds who are ready and willing to obey God and to proclaim the good news of salvation. Imagine a place full of humble, uneducated, low-income servants of God who are willing to live and give for God, die for God, and sacrifice for the sake of God. They travelled a long way, left their flocks, their job, family and homes. Matthew Henry wrote: "We have reason to think that the shepherds told Joseph and Mary of the vision of the angels they had seen, and the song of the angels they had heard, which was a great encouragement to them, more than if a visit had been made them by the best ladies in the town. And it is probable that Joseph and Mary told the shepherds what visions they had had concerning the child; and so, by communicating their experiences to each other, they greatly strengthened one another's faith." (The Bible Collection)

It's so unfortunate to know that many churches would rather close their door to the poor than have them occupy their expensive pews. On that blessed night of Christ's birth, God honored the shepherds who faithfully loved Him and obeyed His call and His Word. We need more lowly shepherds in the mission fields, in the pulpit, and in our churches. They might have been outcasts during their times, but God saw their hearts and their willingness to obey His will. God entrusted to them the message of God to all people: "And the angel said unto them, Fear not: for, behold, I bring you good tidings of great joy, which shall be to all people." (Luke 2:10 KJV)

The world is full of excuses, by people who refused,
To follow God in the way; to serve, and love all the way,
What matters most at the end of the day is what
God has planned for me.

"16- And they came with haste, and found Mary, and Joseph, and the babe lying in a manger. 17-And when they had seen it, they made known abroad the saying which was told them concerning this child. 18- And all they that heard it wondered at those things which were told them by the shepherds." (Luke 2:16- 18 KJV)

What Was on Mary's Mind?

"And I will put enmity between thee and the woman, and between thy seed and her seed; it shall bruise thy head, and thou shalt bruise his heel. 16- Unto the woman he said, I will greatly multiply thy sorrow and thy conception; in sorrow thou shalt bring forth children; and thy desire shall be to thy husband, and he shall rule over thee." (Genesis 3:15- 16 KJV)

If Mary was by your side right now, and she gave you the opportunity to interview her, and ask her some personal questions; what would you ask her? For me, I would ask her: "Mary, what was on your mind twenty-five days before the first Christmas?" And if I would want Mary to think the way I think right now, then I would say; "I was thinking about the first prophecy in the Bible right after the fall of man, and I was thinking about the Savior of the world." Or Mary might say, "I don't even know what God has for me…" She might also think, "How did it happen? Is this a miracle in the process, a blessing, a fortune or what?" "Why have you chosen me Lord, and not Elisabeth or someone else?" And Mary may have said, "I can't believe God was talking about me in His prophecy in Genesis 3:15: "And I will put enmity between thee and the woman, and between thy seed and her seed; it shall bruise thy head, and thou shalt bruise his heel." Those are all my speculations and imaginations, but the truth of the prophecy and its fulfillment will remain, even if you do not believe in Christmas.

The essence and spirit of Christmas was with Mary and Joseph twenty-five days before Christ's birth. It was there already thousands of years before Jesus was even born. What's on her mind and on Joseph's mind, as well as whatever is in people's mind during Christmas day will not matter if Jesus is not the center of your celebration. We could be thinking of money, gifts, parties and other related things regarding Christmas, but God is thinking about you, the forgiveness of our sins, and the eternal life He offers. We believe Jesus was born to save us! He was born to set us free and to give us hope.

> On Christmas day, we laugh and play
> We exchange some gifts then eat and pray,
> The love we share with tears we care
> We know its way better, if Christ is the center.

> "But when the fullness of the time was come,
> God sent forth his Son, made of a woman,
> made under the law." (Galatians 4:4)

It's Not Just an "Infancy Narrative" for God!

Someone said to me years ago that the first two chapters of the book of Matthew are the "infancy narratives" and that's it. I said: "But for me whatever you may call it, it's all about Jesus, God's love, and purpose for mankind. Remember, His birth is for the salvation of all!" What is "infancy" anyways? According to FreeDictionary.Com, infancy means: *"1. The earliest period of childhood, especially before the ability to walk has been acquired. 2. The state of being an infant."* What are narratives? Narratives means *"a message that tells the particulars of an act or occurrence or course of events; presented in writing or drama or cinema or as a radio or television program."* If I put "Christmas as infancy narratives" in my own words as recorded in the book of Matthew chapters One and two, it would be: "The earliest period of the childhood of the Lord Jesus Christ with the acts, occurrences, and course of events as per records, And it's all about Jesus, God's love, and purpose for mankind. His birth is for the salvation of all!" If you don't believe in Christmas, you must at least believe in Christ's birth and call it whatever pleases you, and your church or organization. Just be sure to celebrate its purpose, exercise its goals, and stay focused on what God wants to have accomplished through His birth.

The Chinese and the Jews have their own months and days and ways of celebrating New Years day. I'm not trying to divert the subject from Christmas to New Year. It's about what Paul was saying in the book of Galatians. We are not servants of days and seasons, but we must be looking into the possibilities and opportunities to spread His Word. Notice Paul's writing; "But now, after that ye have known God, or rather are known of God, how turn ye again to the weak and beggarly elements, whereunto ye desire again to be in bondage? 10- Ye observe days, and months, and times, and years. 11- I am afraid of you, lest I have bestowed upon you labour in vain." (Galatians 4:9- 11 KJV)

We can use Christmas to open the door for the gospel of the Lord Jesus Christ. What will you do, and what do you plan to give to Jesus this Christmas season? The world is more religious, pious and nice on Christmas; it means it's easier to share His love and His grace. The unbelieving people are more open to His Word on Christmas. It's so easy to share about Christ because it's His birthday. You may have plans of giving things in relation to His birth, and forget God's thing which is the true message and spirit of Christmas. Worship Him, rejoice with your fellow Christians, present your gifts to God, and bless the name of Jesus!

Is Christmas Just a "Hypothesis"?

Is Christmas just a "hypothesis"? I was asked the same question by a friend, but with arrogance. What I mean is that he had the answer in his mind set up already. What is "hypothesis"? According to Dictionary.com, hypothesis means: "1. *a proposition, or set of propositions, set forth as an explanation for the occurrence of some specified group of phenomena, either asserted merely as a provisional conjecture to guide investigation (working hypothesis) or accepted as highly probable in the light of established facts. 2. a proposition assumed as a premise in an argument. 3. the antecedent of a conditional proposition. 4. A mere assumption or guess."*

The Biblical account of Christmas is very different from what we have today. The world made a lot of changes in the Nativity scenes, the hymns and music, the messages that are being spread out through mass media or via internet. It is very disappointing to read and watch the movies of those who made up their own Christmas stories, and other mythical stories about Christmas. We don't have the exact dates and exact spot where Jesus was born, but we have the truth of one of the greatest events in world history. We have the Word of God that tells us that Christmas was an event, and something that happened more than 2,000 years ago. Christmas is not a man-made event, occurrence, or some kind of phenomenon. It's a fact! The sole truth is written in the Scriptures. If you don't believe in Christmas because there is no word for "Christmas" in the scriptures, then it would be right to believe there is no abortion because you cannot find the word "abortion" in the Scriptures. It is true that you cannot find the word "Christmas" in the scriptures, but the essence, the truth, the event, and the elements of Christmas are as true as the parting of the Red Sea. There's nothing wrong with cultures and traditions, and it's not wrong to practice or celebrate Christmas in the church or with your love ones.

My Baptist pastor friend who was very conservative, a close-minded man, and a man of his own box made a comment to me about my stand regarding Christmas celebration. He said: "Ely, you're not supposed to celebrate Christmas because it is being commercialized." He was partly right! It is obvious that some of the business people from around the world use Christmas for their financial gain. If you remember the classic movie *The Miracle at the 34th Street*, the Macy's store and Santa Claus tried to set up people's perspective about Christmas by not commercializing it. They tell their customers to go to the other stores if they don't have what the customers were looking for, and they even gave them some information regarding the other stores. That's the spirit of Christmas- sharing, not commercializing. I was watching the Radio City Christmas presentation in a video, and I was surprised to see how they portrayed the Christmas story at the later part of the show. At first, I was thinking Radio City was just commercializing Christmas, but I was wrong. The irony is some Christians would not even celebrate Christmas at home or in their churches.

The Biblical Account of Christmas and Our Present Cultures and Traditions

Mr. Kit Acosta (not his real name) shared to me his experiences and observations in the Middle East. Kit was stationed in Saudi Arabia, and he was overwhelmed by the culture of the Muslims and the way they celebrate Christmas on December twenty five. The Muslims in the said country don't celebrate Christmas the way we do as Christians. But if they do, it's still different. Although they believe Jesus Christ as a prophet according to their Quran; celebrating Christ's birth is forbidden. Kit said that they celebrate Mohammed's birthday, but not Jesus' birthday. Although both the Lord Jesus Christ and Mohammed are recognized as prophets by the Muslims, they treated them differently in terms of birthday celebration. Kit is a good Christian, and he celebrated Christmas with foods on the table and played Christmas carols inside their rooms during Christmas seasons. Christmas celebration for Kit with his friends is underground. For Christians to be able to celebrate Christmas freely, they have to go to a place called

ARAMCO, which Kit said is like a private commercial compound. Kit did not specify the place, but he said that the Saudi government does not bother them in their celebration of Christmas if they're inside the said compound. Kit shared to me about the desire of many Muslims to celebrate Christmas as well, but they don't have the freedom to do so. Those who can afford, they would have to fly or drive to the free countries where they would spend their money on Christmas season and celebrate the Nativity. He said, "The wealthy Muslims will either go to the Emirates, Dubai, or fly to London or USA for Christmas."

I'm so grateful to God to be able to live in a free country like the United States of America, United Kingdom or the Philippines. Christians and the whole world celebrate Christmas with different practices, cultures, and traditions. We celebrate Christmas here in the USA differently if compared to those who are on the other side of the world. Start a new tradition in your church. You can try or adopt the new tradition of celebrating Christmas with some of your brethren from the other parts of the world.

In the Philippines; caroling, fireworks, family time, gift giving, beautiful decorations of Christmas trees, lantern and Nativity are a deal. Christmas parties and Christmas bonuses are the common practices and tradition in work places. You would be surprised to hear Christmas carols playing on the radio and in the malls on first week of September. Christmas is a big celebration in the Philippines. A friend of mine from the Philippines posted on her Facebook account about a secular Radio station playing "Hard the

Herald Angels Sing" on September first. We'll we can play Christmas music all year long if we learn to accept and celebrate "Christmas Every Day"!

Midori Takeuchi Thomas is a member of International Community Christian Church of Trenton, Michigan. She shared to me how the Japanese people in Japan celebrate Christmas in a little different way. "Unfortunately," she said, "most of the Japanese people don't know Christianity."

"It is kind of weird because you're celebrating the birthday of someone you don't know. Although they do exchange gifts, believe in Santa Claus, decorate Christmas trees, and sing Christmas carols; they don't know it's the Lord's birthday, and they don't know the meaning of Christmas," she added. Japanese people didn't celebrate Christmas about hundred years ago before Japan was opened to other religions including Christianity. New Years day is more popular and a big celebration in Japan compared to Christmas.

I came across a video clips about Christmas in You Tube. The video was from a church in Sydney, Australia. I thank the Lord for the generosity of Mr. James Chik for letting us use their clips. I hope and pray that you will find these interesting and a blessing. These are some of the things that we use, practiced, and do at Christmas time that others may not even know or have no idea at all.

DID YOU KNOW?

That the German god "ODIN" had a flying horse, "SLEIPNIR". He flew roof to roof and went down the chimneys putting gifts and stockings by the fireplace for children who filled the boots with food for ODIN's horse SLEIPNIR.

DID YOU KNOW? That "YULE" or "YULETIDE" is an ancient European Winter Festival that celebrates the birth of the SUN GODS, it contains many traditions such as:

- Exchanging gifts
- Decorating Christmas trees
- Using holly and wreaths
- Kissing under the mistletoe.

DID YOU KNOW? That the name "SANTA CLAUSE" comes from "SINTERKLAAS" which is a holiday that celebrates "SAINT NICHOLAS", who was a bishop of Turkey that gave gifts to poor children.

DID YOU KNOW? That Australia accumulates $41,000,000,000 of credit card debt after Christmas.

CHRISTMAS

Christ - Mas

Christos - Maesse

God's Annointed Festival or Mass

(From Asian Bible Church, Christmas

Coverage with Will via You Tube)

"The Old Testament begins with the book of the generation of the world, and it is its glory that it does so; but the glory of the New Testament *herein* excelleth, that it begins with *the book of the generation of* him that made the world. As

God, *his outgoings were of old, from everlasting* (Mic. 5:2), and none can declare that generation; but, as man, he was *sent forth in the fulness of time, born of a woman,* and it is that generation which is here declared." (Henry Concise Commentary)

The Messy Christmas and a Mocked King

Indeed, the first Christmas day was filled with anger, doubt, deception, and violence from those who are against it- the devil and his angels. It was a mess to King Herod and his army. When Herod the King had heard these things, he was troubled, and all Jerusalem with him. It was a big mess to parents who lost their children because of Herod's declaration to kill all the children ages two and under. Imagine them running away for their life from King Herod's army. Imagine Mary and Joseph travelling to Egypt with just camels, or donkeys, or maybe with the horses. They came from that little room with Jesus in a manger. Jesus was born with the animals by His side and with Mary and Joseph in a little stinky room with the presence of the Holy Spirit. Months may have passed or maybe more than a year when King Herod sought to kill the children and the babies. They may have been in a small house when they were told by an angel of God to flee. (Matthew 2:11- 23) In human perspective and in man's eyes, it was a mess but for God it was part of His plan and the best has yet to come for the whole world!

We have no idea what was in Herod's heart when he decided to kill the children. If the reason why he killed the children was because he felt he was mocked by the wise men; then the killing is not acceptable to God, to the law of men, and even to any kingdom and form of government. The Bible says; "Then Herod, when he saw that he was mocked of the wise men, was exceeding wroth, and sent forth, and slew all the children that were in Bethlehem, and in all the coasts thereof, from two years old and under, according to the time which he had diligently enquired of the wise men." (Matthew 2:16 KJV) I surely believe it was insecurity, jealousy, envy, or the least is politically motivated killings. We cannot overturn the fulfillment of the Old Testament prophecies according to (Jeremiah 31:15; Hosea 11:1).

The Miracle of Christmas

- Jesus was born of a virgin through the working of the Holy Spirit of God. Whether you believe it or not, the truth will remain.
- The Lord protected Joseph and Mary on their trips and the Lord provided all their needs. (Luke 2:1- 11)
- The Lord was with the wise men. (Matthew 2:1- 2)
- The supernatural appearance of the star of God.
- The miracle and timing of Elisabeth being with child in her old age. The child was named John who will "prepare the way of the Lord." (Luke 2:1- 25)

- Jesus was not killed by the armies of King Herod. The Lord was with them when they fled from Herod's wrath. (Matthew 2:1- 23)
- You are a miracle of God every day and every Christmas season. I have heard of people's faith, forgiveness, reconciliations of families and friends, and healing of all sorts. The Lord is working with us and through us, and He is working miracles in our lives.

The *GREATEST MIRACLE* at the start of the New Testament era was the virgin birth. One of the *GREATEST PURPOSES* that the world witnessed from the birth of our Lord and Savior Jesus Christ was His death on the cross. The purpose of His death was to save us from our sins. One of the *GREATEST MIRACLES after the virgin birth* was the resurrection of the Lord Jesus Christ. He rose from the dead so we can be with Him forever and ever. (John 11:23- 26)

"After the Big Christmas Celebration... What?"

"Even the Spirit of truth; whom the world cannot receive, because it seeth him not, neither knoweth him: but ye know him; for he dwelleth with you, and shall be in you." (John 14:17 KJV)

I was on the Internet just a few minutes before I typed in the topic for Mi Daily Devotion. And I left for a few seconds, and when I came back online, guess what was on the top of Yahoo search? "After Christmas" And I was just thinking about this subject while I was watching TV with my youngest son EJ that night… EJ said something like this; "It will be another 365 days before Christmas," and after a while EJ said, "Now that Christmas is almost over…" EJ was already looking forward of celebrating the next Christmas. We have after-Christmas sales, after-Christmas best deals, after-Christmas sales tips, and the after- Christmas clean ups. After Christmas checking and balancing of credit card debt, and the check and balance of our bank account. Checking on how much you've gained or lost because of so much food and stress. Remember to always keep the spirit of Christmas in our hearts.

The Christmas celebration is on December 25, but the spirit of Christmas must be 24/7, 365 or 366 days a year. Don't leave the spirit of Christmas on the table, in your unwrapped gifts or in your Christmas tree. Keep it in your hearts as you keep the Lord's commandment. We can keep the spirit of Christmas with God's love and our devotion to Him and Him alone. Let His spirit, God's Spirit dwell in *you*. The baby in a manger more than 2,000 years ago changed my life, He changed my heart, He changed my perspective, He changed my way of thinking, He changed my direction and I can go on and on. That little baby did not remain in a manger. He grew up in an "unpleasant place" called Nazareth. He was not a thing, because He was born in a very small city of Bethlehem which means the "house of bread." He grew up as a very wise boy, a little boy who was so full of wisdom and knowledge that even the doctors and lawyers asked questions of Him. (Luke 2:39- 40) If you will just look at this little boy from the manger to Nazareth;

imagine how He would become a good teacher, a healer, a writer and the greatest philanthropist in the world from the time of Adam and Eve up to the present. It's beyond our imagination.

The little baby in that little manger with the sheep and other animals is the Savior of the world. He is the Messiah and the King of kings. He is the one who shaped up my life, and He can do the same to you. He is the one who showed me the way from darkness to glory. He is the one who gave us joy, peace, and satisfaction that this old world can never do. He is the *Christ* of Christmas, the only reason for the season, and the center of the celebration. He is the reason why we have the steadfast love of the Lord. He is the Alpha and Omega, the Beginning and the End. He is the Eternal God, the Second Person of the Holy Trinity and He is the only way, the truth and the life. (John 14:6) "For unto us a child is born, unto us a son is given: and the government shall be upon his shoulder: and his name shall be called Wonderful, Counsellor, The mighty God, The everlasting Father, The Prince of Peace." (Isaiah 9:6 KJV) Jesus said: "I am Alpha and Omega, the beginning and the ending, saith the Lord, which is, and which was, and which is to come, the Almighty." (Revelation 1:8)

Is Christmas something like a pattern for you where you will just walk through it year after year? Are you thinking of doing something different this Christmas or after Christmas? Change is something that will surely hurt even the strongest man in the world. The strongest political group, the fastest growing church, as well as the stagnant church can be hurt with change. The oldest person in the world can be affected by change. What type of change or what do you have to change after Christmas? Is it your heart, your outlook in life or the way you treat and celebrate Christmas? Let God and Christmas help you carry on through beyond what you can do, and may this be the sweetest celebration of the year for *you*!

About the Author

 Reverend Ely R. S. is a graduate of International Baptist Theological College and was the administrator of its extension school for 7 years. He's been a pastor for more than 3 decades. Ely hosted the radio program "Gideon 300" at DWGO AM Radio based in Olongapo City, Philippines. He started the radio program "Love is the Reason" aired on Light House Radio 106.3 FM. He pioneered International Community Christian Church in Trenton, Michigan-(SBC). Ely is the author of four books, and he is the founder, and owner of Mi Daily Devotion. Ely is married to former Vemerlyn Dumala. They were blessed by the Lord with four (4) children; Eliezer, Ely JR, Eliel Lyn and Elmer John (EJ).

Visit his web page and know more about him and check his other books on the internet at www.ely-roque-sagansay.com.

Acknowledgement/Bibliography

Reverend and Mrs. Jimmy Jones

Eliezer Dumala Sagansay- Sponsor

Music Prescription- Sponsor

James Farinas- Art work

International Community Christian Church- 4049 Longmeadow Drive, Trenton, Michigan 48180 USA

First Baptist Church of Trenton, 4049 Longmeadow Drive, Trenton, Michigan 48180 USA

Album "Ten Thousand Years" CD
by Eliezer Dumala Sagansay

C. I. Scofield Bible- KJV 1611

Mi Daily Devotion

Elmer John (EJ) Dumala Sagansay- Typist

The Bible Collection- Software

Wikipedia-Yahoo.com (Internet)

The Free Dictionary on Yahoo (Internet)

Songwriters: Dennis, John Randall / Mohr, Jon
Marvin Gaye and Tammi Terrell (Internet)

Frederick M. Lehman (Internet)

http://www.lyricsmode.com/lyrics/a/
avalonLyrics (Internet)

Dr. J. Vernon McGee - Thru the Bible Books, Box
7100 Pasadena, California 91109, USA

Dr. Billy Graham "Peace with God"

C. A. Chader; Zondervan Publishing House Grand
Rapids, Michigan, Copyright 1938

Unger's Bible Dictionary by Merrill F. Unger,
Moody Press, Chicago Copyright 1957

Yahoo voices (Internet)

Kit Acosta Saudi Arabia

Midori Takeuchi Thomas- Japan- USA

James Chik- From Asian Bible Church, Christmas
Coverage with Will via You Tube (Internet)

Chader, C. A. *God's Plan Through the Ages.* Grand Rapids, MI: Zondervan Publishing House, 1938.

Henry, Matthew. *The Bible Collection.* (Software)

When God Became Man McGee, Dr. J. Vernon-Pasadena, CA: Thru the Bible Books, Unger, Merrill F. *Unger's Bible Dictionary.* Chicago: Moody Press, 1957.

Reverend Felmar Caridad

Photo by: Ely Roque Sagansay

Visit Ely's Web Pages:

www.ely-roque-sagansay.com
Email: esagansay@yahoo.com

Endorsement

Reverend Ely R. S. is a dedicated servant- leader. He is an author with multi-faceted experience easily mirrored and manifested in his writings. You will enjoy his new book "The *New* Christmas Every Day", as it is straight from the Bible and from his heart. Ely is a visionary and a missionary overseer. I highly recommend his new book in your reading agenda. He will take you to new heights and level in your spiritual journey with God. It's great for devotional and meditation.

Reverend Felnar Mario A. Caridad
Master of Arts in Christian Education
RN, BSN
Diploma Certificate in Theology Moody Bible College
Pastor, Universal Christian Church-UCC- (SBC)
Clinton Township, Michigan

The New Christmas Every Day will enlighten your heart and mind of the true and Biblical message of Christmas. Discover and enjoy the power of the Spirit of Christmas 365 days a year. Unfold the various Christmas drama, meaningful Christmas practices and traditional Christmas cultures from the other side of the world.

Ely R. S.

Printed in the United States
By Bookmasters